I Have, Who Has?

MATH

5-6

Written by
Trisha Callella

Editor: Carla Hamaguchi
Cover Illustrator: Corbin Hillam
Production: Moonhee Pak and Carrie Rickmond
Designer: Moonhee Pak
Art Director: Tom Cochrane

Table of Contents

Introduction

I HAVE, WHO HAS is a series of books that provide interactive group activities. The activities consist of game cards that students read and interactively answer. Each card game consists of 40 cards. The game starts when a student reads the first card. The student who has the card with the answer reads his or her card. The game continues in this manner until the last card is read. The last card's question "loops" back to the first card.

This book provides a fun, interactive way for students to practice various math skills. This resource includes over 35 card games that will improve students' listening skills and teach standards-based skills and strategies. The skills covered include:

- Multiplication
- Division
- Square roots and exponents
- Fractions
- Decimals
- Percents
- Addition and Subtraction of Integers
- Geometry Terms
- Coordinate Plane
- Circle Measurements
- Probability

There is also an active listening and enrichment activity included for most games. This component gives students practice in active listening and extends their learning to the application level.

Even better is the fact that there is hardly any prep work required to start these games in your class. Simply make copies of the game cards, cut them apart, and you are ready to go! These engaging games will keep students entertained as they are learning valuable math skills.

ORGANIZATION

There are 40 reproducible cards for each game. The cards are arranged in columns (top to bottom) in the order they will be read by the class. A reproducible active listening and enrichment page follows most sets of game cards. The interactive card games can be used alone or in conjunction with this reproducible page to have students practice active listening, increase active participation, provide enrichment, and extend and transfer the learning and accountability of each student.

INSTRUCTIONS FOR I HAVE, WHO HAS GAME CARDS

1) Photocopy two sets of the game cards. (Each game has four pages of 10 cards each.)

2) Cut apart one set of game cards. Mix up the cards. Pass out at least one card to each student. (There are 40 cards to accommodate large class sizes. If your class size is less than 40, then some students will have two cards. The important thing is that every student has at least one card.)

3) Keep one copy of the game cards as your reference to the correct order. The cards are printed in order in columns from top to bottom and left to right.

4) Have the student with the first game card begin the game by saying *I have the first card. Who has . . . ?* As each student reads a card, monitor your copy to make sure students are reading the cards in the correct order. If students correctly matched each card, then the last card read will "loop" back to the first card.

INSTRUCTIONS FOR ACTIVE LISTENING & ENRICHMENT PAGE

1) This page is optional and is not necessary to play the game.

2) Copy one page for each student or pair of students.

3) Make sure each student has a light-colored crayon or highlighter (not a marker or pencil) to color over the correct boxes as they are read.

4) As each matching card is read, provide time for students to complete the grid or chart at the top of the page. If the game is slow for a particular class, two children can help each other with one reproducible page.

5) Some games require an overhead transparency. For those activities, copy the reproducible on an overhead transparency. Display the transparency as students play the game.

6) Use the answer key on pages 198–204 to check students' answers.

WHAT TO WATCH FOR

1) Students who have difficulty locating the correct boxes on the active listening and enrichment page after the first game (establish familiarity with the format) may have visual discrimination difficulties.

2) Students who have difficulty reading their card at the correct time may have difficulties with attention, hearing, active listening, or the concepts being reinforced.

VARIATIONS

Visual Aids

- For students who are challenged with mental math, pass out one of the following for students to work out the problems: blank paper, dry erase board, or white copy paper slipped into a page protector to be written on with a dry erase marker.
- Have students write the problem they are asking (from their game card) on a dry erase board to hold up while they read their card.
- As each student reads the card, write down what he or she is asking for on an overhead transparency.
- Have students complete the reproducible page with a partner or alone.
- If you are not using the reproducible pages, provide 100 boards for those students challenged by mental math.

Timed Version

1) Follow the instructions to prepare the game cards so that each student has at least one. Play without the reproducible page. Tell students that they will play the game twice. Challenge them to beat their time in the second round.

2) Have students play the same game again the next day. Can they beat their time again? Remember to mix up the cards and redistribute them before each game.

3) The more students play, the better they will understand the concepts covered in each game. They will also develop stronger phrasing and fluency in reading.

Small Groups

1) Photocopy one set of game cards (four pages, 40 cards total) for each small group. Play without the reproducible page.

2) Cut apart the cards, mix them up, and give a set to each group.

3) Have each group play. You can time the groups to encourage them to pay close attention, read quickly, and stay on task. Which group is the fastest?

4) By playing in smaller groups, each student has more cards. This raises the individual accountability, activity, time on task, and reinforcement opportunities per student.

Multiplication Review

I have the **first card.**

Who has the product of 9 × 10?

I have **63.**

Who has the product of 7 × 7?

I have **90.**

Who has the product of 7 × 4?

I have **49.**

Who has the product of 11 × 4?

I have **28.**

Who has the product of 11 × 11?

I have **44.**

Who has the product of 10 × 10?

I have **121.**

Who has the product of 7 × 3?

I have **100.**

Who has the product of 9 × 8?

I have **21.**

Who has the product of 9 × 7?

I have **72.**

Who has the product of 9 × 6?

I Have, Who Has?: Math • 5–6 © 2006 Creative Teaching Press

Multiplication Review

I have **54.**

Who has the product of 11 × 2?

I have **36.**

Who has the product of 11 × 5?

I have **22.**

Who has the product of 12 × 2?

I have **55.**

Who has the product of 9 × 9?

I have **24.**

Who has the product of 9 × 3?

I have **81.**

Who has the product of 12 × 4?

I have **27.**

Who has the product of 12 × 9?

I have **48.**

Who has the product of 10 × 6?

I have **108.**

Who has the product of 12 × 3?

I have **60.**

Who has the product of 11 × 10?

I Have, Who Has? Math • 5–6 © 2006 Creative Teaching Press

Multiplication Review

I have **110.**

Who has the product of 12 × 8?

I have **120.**

Who has the product of 11 × 9?

I have **96.**

Who has the product of 7 × 8?

I have **99.**

Who has the product of 11 × 3?

I have **56.**

Who has the product of 7 × 6?

I have **33.**

Who has the product of 7 × 10?

I have **42.**

Who has the product of 11 × 7?

I have **70.**

Who has the product of 6 × 11?

I have **77.**

Who has the product of 12 × 10?

I have **66.**

Who has the product of 12 × 12?

I Have, Who Has?: Math • 5–6 © 2006 Creative Teaching Press

Multiplication Review

I have **144.**

Who has the product of 11 × 12?

I have **15.**

Who has the product of 2 × 5?

I have **132.**

Who has the product of 7 × 5?

I have **10.**

Who has the product of 11 × 8?

I have **35.**

Who has the product of 9 × 5?

I have **88.**

Who has the product of 5 × 10?

I have **45.**

Who has the product of 12 × 7?

I have **50.**

Who has the product of 5 × 5?

I have **84.**

Who has the product of 5 × 3?

I have **25.**

Who has the first card?

I Have, Who Has?: Math • 5–6 © 2006 Creative Teaching Press

Multiplication Review

Directions: As your classmates identify the answers, write the products in the boxes. Start at the top and go from left to right.

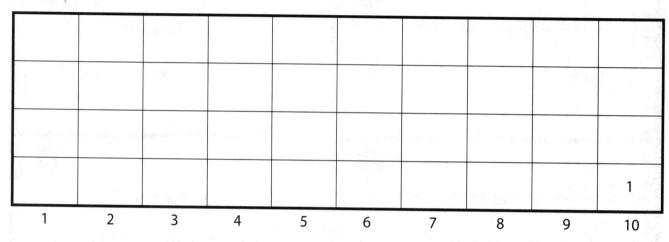

									1
1	2	3	4	5	6	7	8	9	10

Answer the following multiplication questions using the table you created above.

1. The difference between the first and last numbers in Column 1 = 6 × _____.

2. The sum of the first and last numbers in Column 10 = 5 × _____.

3. The difference between the first and last numbers in Column 8 = 5 × _____.

4. The difference between the first number in Column 1 and the last number in Column 2 = 11 × _____.

5. The sum of the last number in Column 2 and the first number in Column 4 = 7 × _____.

6. The sum of the first and last numbers in Column 2 = 7 × _____.

7. The difference between the last number in Column 7 and the first number in Column 2 = 5 × _____.

8. The difference between the last number in Column 4 and the first number in Column 7 = 8 × _____.

9. The sum of the last number in Column 5 and the first number in Column 6 = 8 × _____.

10. The sum of the last numbers in Columns 4 and 5 = 9 × _____.

11. The difference between the last number in Column 4 and the last number in Column 2 = 7 × _____.

12. The difference between the first and last numbers in Column 5 = 6 × _____.

I Have, Who Has?: Math • 5–6 © 2006 Creative Teaching Press

Division Review

Directions: As your classmates identify the answers, highlight each quotient in the hundred chart below.

1	2	3	4	5	6	7	8	9	10
11	12	13	14	15	16	17	18	19	20
21	22	23	24	25	26	27	28	29	30
31	32	33	34	35	36	37	38	39	40
41	42	43	44	45	46	47	48	49	50
51	52	53	54	55	56	57	58	59	60
61	62	63	64	65	66	67	68	69	70
71	72	73	74	75	76	77	78	79	80
81	82	83	84	85	86	87	88	89	90
91	92	93	94	95	96	97	98	99	100

Use the numbers you **highlighted** in the table above to answer the following division questions.

1. The largest number with five ones ÷ 5 = _____.

2. The largest number with two ones ÷ 12 = _____.

3. The largest number with zero ones ÷ 25 = _____.

4. The largest number with three ones ÷ 3 = _____.

5. The largest number with four ones ÷ 11 = _____.

6. The sum of the largest and smallest numbers with five ones ÷ 4 = _____.

7. The sum of the largest and smallest numbers with four ones ÷ 12 = _____.

8. The difference between the largest and smallest numbers with zero ones ÷ 10 = _____.

9. The sum of all highlighted numbers with three ones ÷ 7 = _____.

10. The difference between the highest number and the largest number with five ones ÷ 5 = _____.

11. The sum of all numbers with two tens ÷ 8 = _____.

12. The sum of all numbers with two ones ÷ 9 = _____.

I have the **first card.**

Who has the answer to $5 \times 3 - 1$?

I have **29.**

Who has the answer to $90 \div 3 + 1$?

I have **14.**

Who has the answer to $8 \times 9 - 3$?

I have **31.**

Who has the answer to $50 \times 2 - 9$?

I have **69.**

Who has the answer to $120 \div 12 + 6$?

I have **91.**

Who has the answer to $40 \times 2 - 3$?

I have **16.**

Who has the answer to $75 \div 3 - 7$?

I have **77.**

Who has the answer to $30 \times 3 - 8$?

I have **18.**

Who has the answer to $100 \div 5 + 9$?

I have **82.**

Who has the answer to $81 \div 9 + 4$?

I have **13.**

Who has the answer to 121 ÷ 11 + 9?

I have **58.**

Who has the answer to 8 × 8 − 4?

I have **20.**

Who has the answer to 99 ÷ 11 × 8?

I have **60.**

Who has the answer to 75 ÷ 3 − 2?

I have **72.**

Who has the answer to 120 ÷ 3 + 7?

I have **23.**

Who has the answer to 99 ÷ 11 + 1?

I have **47.**

Who has the answer to 6 × 6 − 9?

I have **10.**

Who has the answer to 8 × 7 − 4?

I have **27.**

Who has the answer to 9 × 6 + 4?

I have **52.**

Who has the answer to 8 × 4 + 6?

I have **38.**

Who has the answer to $6 \times 6 + 20$?

I have **53.**

Who has the answer to $8 \times 8 + 10$?

I have **56.**

Who has the answer to $11 \times 8 - 3$?

I have **74.**

Who has the answer to $40 \div 4 \times 10$?

I have **85.**

Who has the answer to $80 \div 2 + 4$?

I have **100.**

Who has the answer to $63 \div 7 \times 11$?

I have **44.**

Who has the answer to $100 \div 10 \div 2$?

I have **99.**

Who has the answer to $30 \times 2 + 3$?

I have **5.**

Who has the answer to $7 \times 7 + 4$?

I have **63.**

Who has the answer to $30 \times 3 - 3$?

I have **87**.

Who has the answer to $25 \times 4 - 6$?

I have **50**.

Who has the answer to $12 \times 8 - 4$?

I have **94**.

Who has the answer to $100 \div 2 + 1$?

I have **92**.

Who has the answer to $30 \div 2 + 2$?

I have **51**.

Who has the answer to $99 \div 3 + 3$?

I have **17**.

Who has the answer to $7 \times 7 + 10$?

I have **36**.

Who has the answer to $81 \div 9 + 10$?

I have **59**.

Who has the answer to $8 \times 8 - 2$?

I have **19**.

Who has the answer to $75 \div 3 \times 2$?

I have **62**.

Who has the first card?

Basic Operations Mixed Review 1

Directions: As your classmates identify the answers, write the numbers in the boxes. Start at the top and go from left to right.

4									
3									
2									
1									1
	A	B	C	D	E	F	G	H	I	J

Answer the following questions using the completed table above.

1. A1 – A4 ÷ 8 = _____

2. D1 + F4 ÷ 2 = _____

3. H3 × F3 ÷ 100 = _____

4. C1 ÷ 6 × A3 = _____

5. D1 + G1 ÷ C1 = _____

6. A2 ÷ 8 × D2 = _____

7. H2 ÷ 11 × A3 = _____

8. C3 – D3 ÷ D2 = _____

9. G2 ÷ A3 × J4 = _____

10. J2 – G3 ÷ 8 = _____

11. 3(E4) – J2 = _____

12. B4 – A4 ÷ D2 = _____

13. I2 – F4 ÷ C4 = _____

14. J2 + J4 ÷ A3 = _____

15. C3 – D2 – 3(A4) = _____

Answer the following questions based on your answers above.

16. What is the sum of all the answers you wrote above? _____

17. Take that sum and multiply the three digits together. What is your answer? _____

18. Which coordinate in the table above matches your product? _____

I Have, Who Has?: Math • 5–6 © 2006 Creative Teaching Press

I have the **first card.**

Who has the answer to 9 × 9 − 6?

I have **30.**

Who has the answer to 6 × 9 − 2?

I have **75.**

Who has the answer to 7 × 7 + 6?

I have **52.**

Who has the answer to 120 ÷ 12 × 7?

I have **55.**

Who has the answer to 80 ÷ 8 − 7?

I have **70.**

Who has the answer to 84 ÷ 12 × 2?

I have **3.**

Who has the answer to 81 ÷ 9 + 1?

I have **14.**

Who has the answer to 96 ÷ 12 × 8?

I have **10.**

Who has the answer to 9 × 3 + 3?

I have **64.**

Who has the answer to 132 ÷ 11 × 4?

I have **48.**

Who has the answer to 121 ÷ 11 − 6?

I have **95.**

Who has the answer to 6 × 9 + 6?

I have **5.**

Who has the answer to 72 ÷ 8 × 3?

I have **60.**

Who has the answer to 8 × 9 − 10?

I have **27.**

Who has the answer to 100 ÷ 4 + 10?

I have **62.**

Who has the answer to 20 × 3 − 9?

I have **35.**

Who has the answer to 81 ÷ 9 + 20?

I have **51.**

Who has the answer to 11 × 9 − 10?

I have **29.**

Who has the answer to 11 × 8 + 7?

I have **89.**

Who has the answer to 12 × 4 − 5?

I Have, Who Has?: Math • 5–6 © 2006 Creative Teaching Press

Basic Operations Mixed Review 2

I have **43.**

Who has the answer to 20 × 4 − 1?

I have **42.**

Who has the answer to 72 ÷ 9 × 7?

I have **79.**

Who has the answer to 6 × 7 − 20?

I have **56.**

Who has the answer to 30 × 3 + 3?

I have **22.**

Who has the answer to 56 ÷ 7 × 5?

I have **93.**

Who has the answer to 100 ÷ 4 − 10?

I have **40.**

Who has the answer to 27 ÷ 3 × 4?

I have **15.**

Who has the answer to 72 ÷ 12 × 11?

I have **36.**

Who has the answer to 8 × 4 + 10?

I have **66.**

Who has the answer to 6 × 8 + 30?

I Have, Who Has?: Math • 5–6 © 2006 Creative Teaching Press

I have **78.**

Who has the answer to 80 ÷ 4 ÷ 5?

I have **84.**

Who has the answer to 7 × 3 + 10?

I have **4.**

Who has the answer to 25 ÷ 5 × 9?

I have **31.**

Who has the answer to 63 ÷ 9 × 7?

I have **45.**

Who has the answer to 90 ÷ 10 × 9?

I have **49.**

Who has the answer to 56 ÷ 8 × 11?

I have **81.**

Who has the answer to 7 × 7 – 5?

I have **77.**

Who has the answer to 25 × 3 + 1?

I have **44.**

Who has the answer to 8 × 11 – 4?

I have **76.**

Who has the first card?

Basic Operations Mixed Review 2

Directions: As your classmates identify the answers, highlight each number in the hundred chart below.

Z	1	2	3	4	5	6	7	8	9	10
Y	11	12	13	14	15	16	17	18	19	20
X	21	22	23	24	25	26	27	28	29	30
W	31	32	33	34	35	36	37	38	39	40
V	41	42	43	44	45	46	47	48	49	50
U	51	52	53	54	55	56	57	58	59	60
T	61	62	63	64	65	66	67	68	69	70
S	71	72	73	74	75	76	77	78	79	80
R	81	82	83	84	85	86	87	88	89	90
Q	91	92	93	94	95	96	97	98	99	100
	A	B	C	D	E	F	G	H	I	J

Use the numbers you **highlighted** in the table above to answer the following multi-step mental math questions. Each answer will match a number from the table. Write the matching coordinate on the blank lines.

1. The sum of Row Z + BX = _____

2. AR – AW + JZ = _____

3. The highest number in Column J – the lowest number in Row X + DZ = _____

4. The highest number in Row R – the lowest number in Row R + the lowest number in Row Y = _____

5. The highest number in Column B – the lowest number in Column B = _____

6. The highest number in Column J – the lowest number in Column J + EY = _____

7. The highest number in Row T ÷ the highest number in Row Z × the smallest number in Column E = _____

8. The highest number in Row Y ÷ the smallest number in Column E × the smallest number in Row X = _____

9. The sum of Row Y + the highest number in Row V = _____

10. The lowest number in Row R – the lowest number in Column C – the highest number in Row X = _____

I Have, Who Has?: Math • 5–6 © 2006 Creative Teaching Press

Rounding Whole Numbers

I have the **first card**.

Who has 29,901 rounded to the nearest ten thousand?

I have **2,000**.

Who has 45,253 rounded to the nearest ten thousand?

I have **30,000**.

Who has 3,949 rounded to the nearest hundred?

I have **50,000**.

Who has 1,549 rounded to the nearest hundred?

I have **3,900**.

Who has 1,347 rounded to the nearest thousand?

I have **1,500**.

Who has 3,888 rounded to the nearest thousand?

I have **1,000**.

Who has 462 rounded to the nearest ten?

I have **4,000**.

Who has 2,840 rounded to the nearest thousand?

I have **460**.

Who has 1,915 rounded to the nearest thousand?

I have **3,000**.

Who has 7,645 rounded to the nearest thousand?

I Have, Who Has?: Math • 5–6 © 2006 Creative Teaching Press

I have **8,000.**

Who has 832 rounded to the nearest hundred?

I have **7,000.**

Who has 21,560 rounded to the nearest hundred?

I have **800.**

Who has 72,742 rounded to the nearest ten thousand?

I have **21,600.**

Who has 3,124 rounded to the nearest hundred?

I have **70,000.**

Who has 2,505 rounded to the nearest hundred?

I have **3,100.**

Who has 765,752 rounded to the nearest hundred thousand?

I have **2,500.**

Who has 37,099 rounded to the nearest hundred?

I have **800,000.**

Who has 11,987 rounded to the nearest ten thousand?

I have **37,100.**

Who has 7,458 rounded to the nearest thousand?

I have **12,000.**

Who has 136,299 rounded to the nearest hundred thousand?

Rounding Whole Numbers

I have **100,000.**

Who has 64,718 rounded to the nearest thousand?

I have **7,000.**

Who has 1,592,050 rounded to the nearest hundred thousand?

I have **65,000.**

Who has 94,958 rounded to the nearest thousand?

I have **1,600,000.**

Who has 3,505 rounded to the nearest hundred?

I have **95,000.**

Who has 259,032 rounded to the nearest hundred thousand?

I have **3,500.**

Who has 14,636 rounded to the nearest thousand?

I have **300,000.**

Who has 1,351 rounded to the nearest hundred?

I have **15,000.**

Who has 74,765 rounded to the nearest ten thousand?

I have **1,400.**

Who has 6,552 rounded to the nearest thousand?

I have **70,000.**

Who has 3,410 rounded to the nearest hundred?

Rounding Whole Numbers

I have **3,400.**

Who has 3,307 rounded to the nearest ten?

I have **410.**

Who has 4,197 rounded to the nearest hundred?

I have **3,310.**

Who has 1,736 rounded to the nearest hundred?

I have **4,200.**

Who has 16,098 rounded to the nearest ten thousand?

I have **1,700.**

Who has 934,567 rounded to the nearest hundred thousand?

I have **20,000.**

Who has 4,415 rounded to the nearest hundred?

I have **900,000.**

Who has 3,189 rounded to the nearest hundred?

I have **4,400.**

Who has 5,766,077 rounded to the nearest hundred thousand?

I have **3,200.**

Who has 412 rounded to the nearest ten?

I have **5,800,000.**

Who has the first card?

Rounding Whole Numbers

Directions: Highlight each rounded number in the table below as your classmates identify it.

30,000	4,900	500,000	7,000	21,600	3,100	3,400	5,800,000	4,400	20,000
9,000	3,900	1,000	37,100	60,000	3,310	800,000	70,000	410	4,200
2,000	460	5,000	600,000	2,500	1,700	12,000	3,200	15,000	3,500
90,000	50,000	1,500	4,000	1,900	70,000	900,000	100,000	1,400	1,600,000
4,100	4,800	3,000	8,000	800	700,000	65,000	95,000	300,000	7,000

Round each number below. Each answer will be one of the numbers **not** highlighted in the table above.

1. 4,125 = _____ rounded to the nearest hundred

2. 64,559 = _____ rounded to the nearest ten thousand

3. 484,954 = _____ rounded to the nearest hundred thousand

4. 4,943 = _____ rounded to the nearest thousand

5. 1,876 = _____ rounded to the nearest hundred

6. 743,954 = _____ rounded to the nearest hundred thousand

7. 8,958 = _____ rounded to the nearest thousand

8. 94,671 = _____ rounded to the nearest ten thousand

9. 573,042 = _____ rounded to the nearest hundred thousand

10. 4,842 = _____ rounded to the nearest hundred

I Have, Who Has?: Math • 5–6 © 2006 Creative Teaching Press

Rounding Decimals to the Nearest Whole Number

I have the **first card.**

Who has the nearest whole number you would get if you rounded 12.2?

I have **32.**

Who has the nearest whole number you would get if you rounded 1.2?

I have **12.**

Who has the nearest whole number you would get if you rounded 38.5?

I have **1.**

Who has the nearest whole number you would get if you rounded 19.4?

I have **39.**

Who has the nearest whole number you would get if you rounded 5.4?

I have **19.**

Who has the nearest whole number you would get if you rounded 9.8?

I have **5.**

Who has the nearest whole number you would get if you rounded 23.7?

I have **10.**

Who has the nearest whole number you would get if you rounded 21.9?

I have **24.**

Who has the nearest whole number you would get if you rounded 31.8?

I have **22.**

Who has the nearest whole number you would get if you rounded 30.6?

I Have, Who Has? Math • 5–6 © 2006 Creative Teaching Press

Rounding Decimals to the Nearest Whole Number

I have **31.**

Who has the nearest whole number you would get if you rounded 3.7?

I have **7.**

Who has the nearest whole number you would get if you rounded 10.7?

I have **4.**

Who has the nearest whole number you would get if you rounded 28.7?

I have **11.**

Who has the nearest whole number you would get if you rounded 39.9?

I have **29.**

Who has the nearest whole number you would get if you rounded 15.6?

I have **40.**

Who has the nearest whole number you would get if you rounded 13.6?

I have **16.**

Who has the nearest whole number you would get if you rounded 37.9?

I have **14.**

Who has the nearest whole number you would get if you rounded 17.4?

I have **38.**

Who has the nearest whole number you would get if you rounded 7.4?

I have **17.**

Who has the nearest whole number you would get if you rounded 13.1?

I Have, Who Has? Math • 5–6 © 2006 Creative Teaching Press

Rounding Decimals to the Nearest Whole Number

I have **13.**

Who has the nearest whole number you would get if you rounded 20.3?

I have **3.**

Who has the nearest whole number you would get if you rounded 33.3?

I have **20.**

Who has the nearest whole number you would get if you rounded 21.2?

I have **33.**

Who has the nearest whole number you would get if you rounded 24.6?

I have **21.**

Who has the nearest whole number you would get if you rounded 30.1?

I have **25.**

Who has the nearest whole number you would get if you rounded 33.8?

I have **30.**

Who has the nearest whole number you would get if you rounded 36.8?

I have **34.**

Who has the nearest whole number you would get if you rounded 43.6?

I have **37.**

Who has the nearest whole number you would get if you rounded 2.9?

I have **44.**

Who has the nearest whole number you would get if you rounded 28.4?

I Have, Who Has?: Math • 5–6 © 2006 Creative Teaching Press

Rounding Decimals to the Nearest Whole Number

I have **28.**

Who has the nearest whole number you would get if you rounded 1.9?

I have **18.**

Who has the nearest whole number you would get if you rounded 5.7?

I have **2.**

Who has the nearest whole number you would get if you rounded 25.5?

I have **6.**

Who has the nearest whole number you would get if you rounded 35.4?

I have **26.**

Who has the nearest whole number you would get if you rounded 15.2?

I have **35.**

Who has the nearest whole number you would get if you rounded 9.4?

I have **15.**

Who has the nearest whole number you would get if you rounded 7.5?

I have **9.**

Who has the nearest whole number you would get if you rounded 27.1?

I have **8.**

Who has the nearest whole number you would get if you rounded 17.6?

I have **27.**

Who has the first card?

Rounding Decimals to the Nearest Whole Number

Directions: Highlight each rounded whole number in the table below as your classmates identify it.

1	2	3	4	5	6	7	8	9	10
11	12	13	14	15	16	17	18	19	20
21	22	23	24	25	26	27	28	29	30
31	32	33	34	35	36	37	38	39	40
41	42	43	44	45	46	47	48	49	50

Round each of the following decimals to the nearest whole number. Each answer will be one of the numbers **not** highlighted in the table above.

1. 35.7 = _____

2. 42.4 = _____

3. 47.6 = _____

4. 22.9 = _____

5. 46.4 = _____

6. 47.3 = _____

7. 48.6 = _____

8. 40.8 = _____

9. 45.2 = _____

10. 42.6 = _____

Solve the following mental math rounding problems.

11. Start with two dozen. Round it to the nearest ten. Double it. Divide by 10. Multiply by 9. Round to the nearest ten. What is your answer?

    _____

12. Start with the number of ounces in a pound. Round to the nearest ten. Add 5. Multiply by 3. Round to the nearest ten. Add a half dozen. Round to the nearest ten. What is your answer?

    _____

Rounding Decimals to the Nearest Tenth

I have the first card. Who has the number for 8.22 rounded to the nearest tenth?	I have **8.9.** Who has the number for 5.91 rounded to the nearest tenth?
I have **8.2.** Who has the number for 5.51 rounded to the nearest tenth?	I have **5.9.** Who has the number for 7.42 rounded to the nearest tenth?
I have **5.5.** Who has the number for 2.28 rounded to the nearest tenth?	I have **7.4.** Who has the number for 9.63 rounded to the nearest tenth?
I have **2.3.** Who has the number for 10.87 rounded to the nearest tenth?	I have **9.6.** Who has the number for 5.23 rounded to the nearest tenth?
I have **10.9.** Who has the number for 8.94 rounded to the nearest tenth?	I have **5.2.** Who has the number for 10.59 rounded to the nearest tenth?

I have **10.6.**

Who has the number for 2.52 rounded to the nearest tenth?

I have **3.5.**

Who has the number for 8.49 rounded to the nearest tenth?

I have **2.5.**

Who has the number for 6.48 rounded to the nearest tenth?

I have **8.5.**

Who has the number for 6.23 rounded to the nearest tenth?

I have **6.5.**

Who has the number for 7.09 rounded to the nearest tenth?

I have **6.2.**

Who has the number for 2.22 rounded to the nearest tenth?

I have **7.1.**

Who has the number for 2.11 rounded to the nearest tenth?

I have **2.2.**

Who has the number for 3.16 rounded to the nearest tenth?

I have **2.1.**

Who has the number for 3.48 rounded to the nearest tenth?

I have **3.2.**

Who has the number for 3.26 rounded to the nearest tenth?

Rounding Decimals to the Nearest Tenth

I have **3.3.**

Who has the number for 8.37 rounded to the nearest tenth?

I have **7.8.**

Who has the number for 2.59 rounded to the nearest tenth?

I have **8.4.**

Who has the number for 6.25 rounded to the nearest tenth?

I have **2.6.**

Who has the number for 9.47 rounded to the nearest tenth?

I have **6.3.**

Who has the number for 2.41 rounded to the nearest tenth?

I have **9.5.**

Who has the number for 6.39 rounded to the nearest tenth?

I have **2.4.**

Who has the number for 1.38 rounded to the nearest tenth?

I have **6.4.**

Who has the number for 7.61 rounded to the nearest tenth?

I have **1.4.**

Who has the number for 7.81 rounded to the nearest tenth?

I have **7.6.**

Who has the number for 9.02 rounded to the nearest tenth?

I Have, Who Has?: Math • 5–6 • © 2006 Creative Teaching Press

Rounding Decimals to the Nearest Tenth

I have **9.0.**

Who has the number for 1.64 rounded to the nearest tenth?

I have **5.7.**

Who has the number for 2.91 rounded to the nearest tenth?

I have **1.6.**

Who has the number for 7.68 rounded to the nearest tenth?

I have **2.9.**

Who has the number for 7.26 rounded to the nearest tenth?

I have **7.7.**

Who has the number for 8.71 rounded to the nearest tenth?

I have **7.3.**

Who has the number for 1.46 rounded to the nearest tenth?

I have **8.7.**

Who has the number for 3.89 rounded to the nearest tenth?

I have **1.5.**

Who has the number for 1.29 rounded to the nearest tenth?

I have **3.9.**

Who has the number for 5.69 rounded to the nearest tenth?

I have **1.3.**

Who has the first card?

Rounding Decimals to the Nearest Tenth

Directions: As your classmates identify the answers, write the rounded decimals in the boxes. Start at the top and go from left to right.

I										
	L	L	C	R	A	C	U	T	A	O
II										
	G	H	M	A	I	S	T	L	O	R
III										
	E	I	Q	E	L	U	T	V	A	N
IV										1.0
	C	G	E	N	T	E	A	R	E	P

Now rewrite the decimals in each row in order from smallest to largest. Also, rewrite the letter that goes with each decimal to reveal a math-related word in each row.

I										
II										
III										
IV										

I Have, Who Has?: Math • 5–6 © 2006 Creative Teaching Press

I have the **first card.**

Who has 4^2?

I have **121.**

Who has $2^2 - 1$?

I have **16.**

Who has $\sqrt{36}$?

I have **3.**

Who has $\sqrt{144}$?

I have **6.**

Who has $11^2 + 1$?

I have **12.**

Who has $5^2 - 1$?

I have **122.**

Who has $6^2 - 1$?

I have **24.**

Who has 9^2?

I have **35.**

Who has 11^2?

I have **81.**

Who has $\sqrt{64}$?

Square Roots and Exponents—
Numerical Format

I have **8**.

Who has $4^2 - 1$?

I have **82**.

Who has 5^2?

I have **15**.

Who has 2^2?

I have **25**.

Who has $10^2 - 1$?

I have **4**.

Who has $\sqrt{49}$?

I have **99**.

Who has $\sqrt{81}$?

I have **7**.

Who has $2^2 + 1$?

I have **9**.

Who has $5^2 + 1$?

I have **5**.

Who has $9^2 + 1$?

I have **26**.

Who has 8^2?

I Have, Who Has?: Math • 5–6 © 2006 Creative Teaching Press

I have **64.**

Who has $\sqrt{400}$?

I have **48.**

Who has $\sqrt{100} + 5$?

I have **20.**

Who has $3^2 + 1$?

I have **15.**

Who has $8^2 - 1$?

I have **10.**

Who has 6^2?

I have **63.**

Who has $3^2 + 10$?

I have **36.**

Who has $5^2 + 2$?

I have **19.**

Who has $\sqrt{121}$?

I have **27.**

Who has $7^2 - 1$?

I have **11.**

Who has $10^2 + 1$?

I have **101.**

Who has $4^2 + 1$?

I have **49.**

Who has $6^2 + 1$?

I have **17.**

Who has $\sqrt{4}$?

I have **37.**

Who has $12^2 + 1$?

I have **2.**

Who has $7^2 + 1$?

I have **145.**

Who has $8^2 + 1$?

I have **50.**

Who has 12^2?

I have **65.**

Who has 10^2?

I have **144.**

Who has 7^2?

I have **100.**

Who has the first card?

I Have, Who Has?: Math • 5–6 © 2006 Creative Teaching Press

Square Roots and Exponents—Numerical Format

Directions: As your classmates identify the answers, write the numbers in the boxes. Start at the top and go from left to right.

	A	B	C	D	E	F	G	H	I	J
Z										
Y										
X										
W										22

Use the completed chart to answer the questions.

1. What is BW squared? _____

2. What is the square root of DW? _____

3. What is the square root of EW? _____

4. What is the square root of IW? _____

5. What is the square root of AZ? _____

6. What is CY squared? _____

7. What is FZ raised to the third power? _____

8. What is the square root of IZ? _____

9. What is the square root of JY? _____

10. What is GZ squared? _____

11. What is the square root of EZ? _____

12. What is HY squared? _____

I Have, Who Has? Math • 5–6 © 2006 Creative Teaching Press

I have the **first card.**

Who has two raised to the second power?

I have **1,000.**

Who has five raised to the second power?

I have **4.**

Who has four squared plus one?

I have **25.**

Who has three cubed?

I have **17.**

Who has nine raised to the second power?

I have **27.**

Who has the square root of nine?

I have **81.**

Who has ten squared minus one?

I have **3.**

Who has one raised to the third power?

I have **99.**

Who has ten raised to the third power?

I have **1.**

Who has eleven squared?

I Have, Who Has?: Math • 5–6 © 2006 Creative Teaching Press

Square Roots and Exponents— Written Word Format

I have **121**.

Who has one more than seven squared?

I have **26**.

Who has five raised to the third power?

I have **50**.

Who has the square root of eighty-one?

I have **125**.

Who has the square root of one hundred forty-four?

I have **9**.

Who has the square root of twenty-five?

I have **12**.

Who has three more than four squared?

I have **5**.

Who has four raised to the second power?

I have **19**.

Who has ten squared plus one?

I have **16**.

Who has one more than five squared?

I have **101**.

Who has the square root of sixty-four?

I have **8.**

Who has the square root of
sixteen plus two?

I have **0.**

Who has ten less than eight
raised to the second power.

I have **6.**

Who has five less than
five cubed?

I have **54.**

Who has the square root of
forty-nine?

I have **120.**

Who has ten raised to the
fourth power?

I have **7.**

Who has ten raised to the
first power?

I have **10,000.**

Who has one more than
nine squared?

I have **10.**

Who has ten more than two
raised to the third power?

I have **82.**

Who has zero cubed?

I have **18.**

Who has one more than
six squared?

I Have, Who Has?: Math • 5–6 © 2006 Creative Teaching Press

I have **37.**

Who has two less than
eight squared?

I have **11.**

Who has one more than
six squared?

I have **62.**

Who has four less than the
square root of thirty-six?

I have **37.**

Who has seven squared?

I have **2.**

Who has ten more than
five squared?

I have **49.**

Who has one more than
three cubed?

I have **35.**

Who has three more than the
square root of one hundred?

I have **28.**

Who has seven more than the
square root of one hundred?

I have **13.**

Who has the square root of
one hundred twenty-one?

I have **17.**

Who has the first card?

Square Roots and Exponents Written Word Format

Directions: As your classmates identify the answers, write the numbers in the boxes. Start at the top and go from left to right.

Z									
Y									
X									
W									44
	A	B	C	D	E	F	G	H	I	J

Use the completed chart to answer the questions.

1. What is AX squared? _____

2. What is HZ cubed? _____

3. What is the square root of JZ? _____

4. What is the square root of CZ? _____

5. What is EW squared? _____

6. What is GX squared? _____

7. What is the square root of FZ? _____

8. What is the square root of DY? _____

9. What is BW cubed? _____

10. What is BW raised to the fourth power? _____

11. What is the square root of GW? _____

12. What is BY squared? _____

13. What is AZ squared? _____

14. What is CY cubed? _____

15. What is IZ raised to the fourth power? _____

I Have, Who Has?: Math • 5–6 © 2006 Creative Teaching Press

I have the **first card.**

Who has 2×10^2?

I have **500.**

Who has 8×10^2?

I have **200.**

Who has 3×10^4?

I have **800.**

Who has 34×10^2?

I have **30,000.**

Who has 14×10^2?

I have **3,400.**

Who has 4×10^2?

I have **1,400.**

Who has 92×10^2?

I have **400.**

Who has 15×10^2?

I have **9,200.**

Who has 5×10^2?

I have **1,500.**

Who has 13×10^2?

Multiplying by an Exponent of Ten

I have **1,300.**

Who has 51×10^3?

I have **8,000.**

Who has 2×10^3?

I have **51,000.**

Who has 63×10^2?

I have **2,000.**

Who has 9×10^2?

I have **6,300.**

Who has 3×10^2?

I have **900.**

Who has 12×10^3?

I have **300.**

Who has 47×10^3?

I have **12,000.**

Who has 5×10^4?

I have **47,000.**

Who has 8×10^3?

I have **50,000.**

Who has 7×10^2?

I Have, Who Has?: Math • 5–6 © 2006 Creative Teaching Press

I have **700.**

Who has 6×10^2?

I have **1,700.**

Who has 5×10^3?

I have **600.**

Who has 9×10^3?

I have **5,000.**

Who has 16×10^2?

I have **9,000.**

Who has 6×10^4?

I have **1,600.**

Who has 3×10^3?

I have **60,000.**

Who has 11×10^2?

I have **3,000.**

Who has 12×10^2?

I have **1,100.**

Who has 17×10^2?

I have **1,200.**

Who has 9×10^4?

I Have, Who Has?: Math • 5–6 © 2006 Creative Teaching Press

Multiplying by an Exponent of Ten

I have **90,000.**

Who has 6×10^3?

I have **13,000.**

Who has 3×10^4?

I have **6,000.**

Who has 4×10^3?

I have **30,000.**

Who has 14×10^3?

I have **4,000.**

Who has 15×10^3?

I have **14,000.**

Who has 4×10^4?

I have **15,000.**

Who has 7×10^3?

I have **40,000.**

Who has 9×10^2?

I have **7,000.**

Who has 13×10^3?

I have **900.**

Who has the first card?

I Have, Who Has?: Math • 5–6 © 2006 Creative Teaching Press

Multiplying by an Exponent of Ten

Directions: As your classmates identify the answers, write the numbers in the boxes. Start at the top and go from left to right.

									*

Use the completed chart to answer the questions.

1. Write the biggest number from the chart above as an equation multiplied by an exponent of ten.

_____

2. Write the smallest number from the chart above as an equation multiplied by an exponent of ten.

_____

3. Write your age multiplied by ten raised to the third power. _____

4. Write your favorite television channel multiplied by ten cubed. _____

5. Write your classroom number multiplied by ten squared. _____

I Have, Who Has?: Math • 5–6 © 2006 Creative Teaching Press

Identifying Multiples and Factors

I have the **first card.**

Who has three multiples of seven?

I have **1, 33, 3, and 11.**

Who has the first
three multiples of 25?

I have **14, 21, and 28.**

Who has the first
three multiples of three?

I have **25, 50, and 75.**

Who has the factors of 20?

I have **3, 6, and 9.**

Who has the factors of 24?

I have **1, 2, 10, 4, 5, and 20.**

Who has the first
three multiples of 100?

I have **1, 24, 2, 12, 3, 8, 4, and 6.**

Who has the first
three multiples of 5?

I have **100, 200, and 300.**

Who has the factors of 25?

I have **5, 10, and 15.**

Who has the factors of 33?

I have **1, 25, and 5.**

Who has three multiples of 9?

I Have, Who Has?: Math • 5–6 © 2006 Creative Teaching Press

Identifying Multiples and Factors

I have **18, 27, and 36.**

Who has the factors of 100?

I have **1, 36, 2, 18, 3, 12, 4, 9, and 6.**

Who has the first three multiples of ten?

I have **1, 100, 2, 50, 4, 25, 5, 20, and 10.**

Who has the first three multiples of 12?

I have **10, 20, and 30.**

Who has the first three multiples of 6?

I have **12, 24, and 36.**

Who has the factors of 30?

I have **6, 12, and 18.**

Who has the factors of 40?

I have **1, 30, 2, 15, 3, 10, 5, and 6.**

Who has the first three multiples of 20?

I have **1, 40, 2, 20, 4, 10, 5, and 8.**

Who has the factors of 50?

I have **20, 40, and 60.**

Who has the factors of 36?

I have **1, 50, 2, 25, 5, and 10.**

Who has the first three multiples of 50?

Identifying Multiples and Factors

I have **50, 100, and 150.**

Who has the factors of 12?

I have **4, 8, and 12.**

Who has three multiples of 16?

I have **1, 12, 2, 6, 3, and 4.**

Who has the factors of 18?

I have **32, 48, and 64.**

Who has the factors of 35?

I have **1, 18, 2, 9, 3, and 6.**

Who has the first
three multiples of 15?

I have **1, 35, 5, and 7.**

Who has the factors of 60?

I have **15, 30, and 45.**

Who has the factors of 9?

I have **1, 60, 2, 30,
3, 20, 4, 15, 5, 12, 6, and 10.**

Who has the first three
multiples of 8?

I have **1, 3, and 9.**

Who has the first
three multiples of 4?

I have **8, 16, and 24.**

Who has the factors of 16?

I Have, Who Has?: Math • 5–6 © 2006 Creative Teaching Press

Identifying Multiples and Factors

I have **1, 16, 2, 8, and 4.**

Who has three multiples of 200?

I have **1, 45, 3, 15, 5, and 9.**

Who has the factors of 10?

I have **400, 600, and 800.**

Who has three multiples of 11?

I have **1, 10, 2, and 5.**

Who has the factors of 14?

I have **22, 33, and 44.**

Who has the factors of 22?

I have **1, 14, 2, and 7.**

Who has the first
three multiples of 30?

I have **1, 22, 2, and 11.**

Who has the factors of 75?

I have **30, 60, and 90.**

Who has three multiples of 33?

I have **1, 75, 3, 25, 5, and 15.**

Who has the factors of 45?

I have **66, 99, and 330.**

Who has the first card?

I Have, Who Has? Math • 5–6 © 2006 Creative Teaching Press

Identifying Multiples and Factors

Directions: Follow the path by highlighting the answers as your classmates identify them.

START ✪	14 21 28	1, 12, 2, 6, 3, 4	40 60 80	100 200 300	1 25 5	30 45 60	1, 22, 2, 11	1, 75, 3, 25, 5, 15	1, 45, 3, 15, 5, 9
1, 16, 2, 8, 4	3 6 9	1, 24, 2, 12, 3, 8, 4, 6	5 10 15	1, 2, 10, 4, 5, 20	18 27 36	8 12 16	22 33 44	400 600 800	1, 10, 2, 5
1, 22, 2, 11	66, 99, 330	400 600 800 ·	1, 33, 3, 11	25 50 75	1, 100, 2, 50, 4, 25, 5, 20, 10	14 21 28	8 16 24	1, 16, 2, 8, 4	1, 14, 2, 7
1, 30, 2, 15, 3, 10, 5, 6	32 48 64	60 90 120	22 33 44	1, 30, 2, 15, 3, 10, 5, 6	12 24 36	32 48 64	1, 60, 2, 30, 3, 20, 4, 15, 5, 12, 6, 10	1, 50, 2, 25, 5, 10	30 60 90
1, 40, 2, 20, 4, 10, 5, 8	6 12 18	10 20 30	1, 36, 2, 18, 3, 12, 4, 9, 6	20 40 60	1, 14, 2, 7	32 48 64	1, 35, 5, 7	40 60 80	66, 99, 330
1, 50, 2, 25, 5, 10	50 100 150	1, 12, 2, 6, 3, 4	1, 18, 2, 9, 3, 6	15 30 45	1 3 9	4 8 12	1, 45, 3, 15, 5, 9	1, 16, 2, 8, 4	FINISH ✪

Choose five highlighted squares from above. Write whether the numbers are factors or multiples and determine what number they are factors or multiples of.

1._____

2._____

3._____

4._____

5._____

I Have, Who Has?: Math • 5–6 © 2006 Creative Teaching Press

I have the first card.

Who has the least common multiple of 4 and 6?

I have 20.

Who has the least common multiple of 2 and 10?

I have 24.

Who has the least common multiple of 5 and 8?

I have 10.

Who has the least common multiple of 5 and 12?

I have 40.

Who has the least common multiple of 5 and 6?

I have 60.

Who has the least common multiple of 3 and 14?

I have 30.

Who has the least common multiple of 12 and 16?

I have 42.

Who has the least common multiple of 3 and 6?

I have 48.

Who has the least common multiple of 4 and 5?

I have 6.

Who has the least common multiple of 9 and 12?

I Have, Who Has?: Math • 5–6 © 2006 Creative Teaching Press

Least Common Multiple and Greatest Common Factor

I have **36.**

Who has the least common multiple of 6 and 9?

I have **21.**

Who has the least common multiple of 4 and 22?

I have **18.**

Who has the least common multiple of 5 and 7?

I have **44.**

Who has the least common multiple of 32 and 64?

I have **35.**

Who has the least common multiple of 4 and 7?

I have **64.**

Who has the least common multiple of 8 and 9?

I have **28.**

Who has the least common multiple of 11 and 55?

I have **72.**

Who has the least common multiple of 5 and 25?

I have **55.**

Who has the least common multiple of 3 and 7?

I have **25.**

Who has the least common multiple of 72 and 144?

I Have, Who Has?: Math • 5–6 © 2006 Creative Teaching Press

Least Common Multiple and Greatest Common Factor

I have **144.**

Who has the greatest common factor of 21 and 28?

I have **5.**

Who has the greatest common factor of 22 and 55?

I have **7.**

Who has the greatest common factor of 9 and 36?

I have **11.**

Who has the greatest common factor of 22 and 66?

I have **9.**

Who has the greatest common factor of 24 and 36?

I have **22.**

Who has the greatest common factor of 6 and 9?

I have **12.**

Who has the greatest common factor of 6 and 8?

I have **3.**

Who has the greatest common factor of 45 and 60?

I have **2.**

Who has the greatest common factor of 10 and 15?

I have **15.**

Who has the greatest common factor of 12 and 16?

Least Common Multiple and Greatest Common Factor

I have **4**.

Who has the greatest common factor of 13 and 39?

I have **8**.

Who has the greatest common factor of 17 and 34?

I have **13**.

Who has the greatest common factor of 14 and 28?

I have **17**.

Who has the greatest common factor of 50 and 100?

I have **14**.

Who has the greatest common factor of 4 and 23?

I have **50**.

Who has the greatest common factor of 19 and 57?

I have **1**.

Who has the greatest common factor of 16 and 32?

I have **19**.

Who has the greatest common factor of 100 and 200?

I have **16**.

Who has the greatest common factor of 8 and 64?

I have **100**.

Who has the first card?

I Have, Who Has?: Math • 5–6 © 2006 Creative Teaching Press

Least Common Multiple and Greatest Common Factor

Directions: As your classmates identify the answers, write the numbers in the boxes. Start at the top and go from left to right.

START								
	R	W	H	O	E	N	I	X	B
	E	K	T	U	I	M	C	J	H	S
	U	S	F	Y	I	A	R	J	Z	J
	N	R	O	W	U	Y	F	A	N	R

Look at the numbers you wrote. Write the numbers that are multiples of 5 in the boxes below. Go from top to bottom and left to right. Write the letter that corresponds with each number to reveal the answer to the riddle:

When can you put pickles in a door?

Numbers												
Letters												

Answer: _____

Equivalent Fractions

I have the **first card.**

Who has a fraction
equivalent to ⅑?

I have ⁸⁸/₁₂₁.

Who has a fraction
equivalent to ²/₇?

I have ²/₁₈.

Who has a fraction
equivalent to ⁴/₁₁?

I have ²⁰/₇₀.

Who has a fraction
equivalent to ¹/₁₅?

I have ²⁰/₅₅.

Who has a fraction
equivalent to ⅝?

I have ²/₃₀.

Who has a fraction
equivalent to ⅕?

I have ¹⁰/₁₆.

Who has a fraction
equivalent to ⅙?

I have ²/₁₀.

Who has a fraction
equivalent to ²/₁₅?

I have ⁵/₃₀.

Who has a fraction
equivalent to ⁸/₁₁?

I have ²⁰/₁₅₀.

Who has a fraction
equivalent to ⁵/₇?

I Have, Who Has?: Math • 5–6 © 2006 Creative Teaching Press

Equivalent Fractions

I have ¹⁰⁄₁₄.

Who has a fraction
equivalent to ⁴⁄₇?

I have ⁷⁰⁄₁₀₀.

Who has a fraction
equivalent to ¹⁄₁₁?

I have ¹⁶⁄₂₈.

Who has a fraction
equivalent to ¹⁄₁₂?

I have ¹⁰⁄₁₁₀.

Who has a fraction
equivalent to ⁴⁄₅?

I have ⁵⁄₆₀.

Who has a fraction
equivalent to ½?

I have ⁸⁰⁄₁₀₀.

Who has a fraction
equivalent to ⁵⁄₁₂?

I have ⁵⁰⁄₁₀₀.

Who has a fraction
equivalent to ⁷⁄₁₁?

I have ⁶⁰⁄₁₄₄.

Who has a fraction
equivalent to ⅔?

I have ⁴⁹⁄₇₇.

Who has a fraction
equivalent to ⁷⁄₁₀?

I have ⁶⁰⁄₉₀.

Who has a fraction
equivalent to ⁵⁄₁₁?

I Have, Who Has? Math • 5–6 © 2006 Creative Teaching Press

Equivalent Fractions

I have ²⁵/₅₅.

Who has a fraction
equivalent to ³/₇?

I have ³³/₁₂₁.

Who has a fraction
equivalent to ¼?

I have ¹²/₂₈.

Who has a fraction
equivalent to ²/₁₁?

I have ²⁵/₁₀₀.

Who has a fraction
equivalent to ²/₉?

I have ²⁰/₁₁₀.

Who has a fraction
equivalent to ³/₁₀?

I have ⁶/₂₇.

Who has a fraction
equivalent to ³/₅?

I have ⁶/₂₀.

Who has a fraction
equivalent to ¾?

I have ⁶⁰/₁₀₀.

Who has a fraction
equivalent to ⁹/₁₁?

I have ⁷⁵/₁₀₀.

Who has a fraction
equivalent to ³/₁₁?

I have ⁸¹/₉₉.

Who has a fraction
equivalent to ¹/₁₀?

I Have, Who Has?: Math • 5–6 © 2006 Creative Teaching Press

Equivalent Fractions

I have $\frac{10}{100}$.

Who has a fraction equivalent to $\frac{1}{3}$?

I have $\frac{18}{20}$.

Who has a fraction equivalent to $\frac{2}{5}$?

I have $\frac{2}{6}$.

Who has a fraction equivalent to $\frac{10}{11}$?

I have $\frac{40}{100}$.

Who has a fraction equivalent to $\frac{5}{6}$?

I have $\frac{30}{33}$.

Who has a fraction equivalent to $\frac{1}{8}$?

I have $\frac{35}{42}$.

Who has a fraction equivalent to $\frac{4}{15}$?

I have $\frac{5}{40}$.

Who has a fraction equivalent to $\frac{6}{11}$?

I have $\frac{8}{30}$.

Who has a fraction equivalent to $\frac{1}{7}$?

I have $\frac{30}{55}$.

Who has a fraction equivalent to $\frac{9}{10}$?

I have $\frac{9}{63}$.

Who has the first card?

Equivalent Fractions

Directions: As your classmates identify the answers, write the fractions in the boxes. Start at the top and go from left to right.

									$^5/_7$

Write three equivalent fractions for the first and last fractions you wrote in each row above.

1._____ = _____ = _____ = _____

2._____ = _____ = _____ = _____

3._____ = _____ = _____ = _____

4._____ = _____ = _____ = _____

5._____ = _____ = _____ = _____

6._____ = _____ = _____ = _____

7._____ = _____ = _____ = _____

8._____ = _____ = _____ = _____

Reducing Fractions

I have the **first card.**

Who has ⁹⁰⁄₁₀₀ reduced to the simplest form?

I have ½.

Who has ⁹⁄₂₄ reduced to the simplest form?

I have ⁹⁄₁₀.

Who has ²⁵⁄₃₅ reduced to the simplest form?

I have ⅜.

Who has ¹¹⁄₁₁₀ reduced to the simplest form?

I have ⁵⁄₇.

Who has ⁶⁶⁄₉₉ reduced to the simplest form?

I have ¹⁄₁₀.

Who has ¹⁵⁄₃₅ reduced to the simplest form?

I have ⅔.

Who has ²²⁄₅₀ reduced to the simplest form?

I have ³⁄₇.

Who has ⁶⁄₁₀ reduced to the simplest form?

I have ¹¹⁄₂₅.

Who has ⁹⁄₁₈ reduced to the simplest form?

I have ⅗.

Who has ²⁰⁄₉₀ reduced to the simplest form?

Reducing Fractions

I have ²/₉.

Who has ¹⁶/₁₀₀ reduced to the simplest form?

I have ⁴/₅.

Who has ²⁵/₃₀ reduced to the simplest form?

I have ⁴/₂₅.

Who has ³/₁₂ reduced to the simplest form?

I have ⁵/₆.

Who has ⁸/₂₈ reduced to the simplest form?

I have ¼.

Who has ¹⁰/₂₅ reduced to the simplest form?

I have ²/₇.

Who has ³⁰/₁₀₀ reduced to the simplest form?

I have ²/₅.

Who has ¹⁰/₈₀ reduced to the simplest form?

I have ³/₁₀.

Who has ⁸/₂₄ reduced to the simplest form?

I have ⅛.

Who has ¹⁶/₂₀ reduced to the simplest form?

I have ⅓.

Who has ¹⁰/₁₂₀ reduced to the simplest form?

I Have, Who Has?: Math • 5–6 © 2006 Creative Teaching Press

Reducing Fractions

I have ¹/₁₂.

Who has ²/₅₀ reduced to the simplest form?

I have ⅙.

Who has ⁹/₆₃ reduced to the simplest form?

I have ¹/₂₅.

Who has ¹⁶/₃₆ reduced to the simplest form?

I have ⅐.

Who has ²/₃₀ reduced to the simplest form?

I have ⁴/₉.

Who has ²⁰/₁₀₀ reduced to the simplest form?

I have ¹/₁₅.

Who has ¹⁴/₂₀ reduced to the simplest form?

I have ⅕.

Who has ⁷⁵/₁₀₀ reduced to the simplest form?

I have ⁷/₁₀.

Who has ⁵⁰/₈₀ reduced to the simplest form?

I have ¾.

Who has ⁵/₃₀ reduced to the simplest form?

I have ⅝.

Who has ⁵⁴/₆₃ reduced to the simplest form?

Reducing Fractions

I have ⁶⁄₇.

Who has ⁷⁄₆₃ reduced to the simplest form?

I have ¹⁄₁₃.

Who has ⁴⁹⁄₅₆ reduced to the simplest form?

I have ¹⁄₉.

Who has ⁴⁄₃₀ reduced to the simplest form?

I have ⅞.

Who has ¹⁶⁄₂₈ reduced to the simplest form?

I have ²⁄₁₅.

Who has ¹⁰⁄₂₄ reduced to the simplest form?

I have ⁴⁄₇.

Who has ²¹⁄₃₆ reduced to the simplest form?

I have ⁵⁄₁₂.

Who has ³²⁄₃₆ reduced to the simplest form?

I have ⁷⁄₁₂.

Who has ²⁵⁄₄₅ reduced to the simplest form?

I have ⁸⁄₉.

Who has ²⁄₂₆ reduced to the simplest form?

I have ⁵⁄₉.

Who has the first card?

I Have, Who Has?: Math • 5–6 © 2006 Creative Teaching Press

Reducing Fractions

Directions: As your classmates identify the answers, write the fractions in the boxes. Start at the top and go from left to right.

								³⁄₈

Write three equivalent fractions for the first and last fractions you wrote in each row above.

1._____ = _____ = _____ = _____

2._____ = _____ = _____ = _____

3._____ = _____ = _____ = _____

4._____ = _____ = _____ = _____

5._____ = _____ = _____ = _____

6._____ = _____ = _____ = _____

7._____ = _____ = _____ = _____

8._____ = _____ = _____ = _____

Changing Improper Fractions
to Mixed Numbers

I have the **first card**.

Who has the mixed
number for ¹⁶⁄₅?

I have **4½**.

Who has the mixed
number for ¹¹⁄₅?

I have **3⅕**.

Who has the mixed
number for ⁵⁄₂?

I have **2⅕**.

Who has the mixed
number for ¹³⁄₆?

I have **2½**.

Who has the mixed
number for ¹⁰⁄₃?

I have **2⅙**.

Who has the mixed
number for ²³⁄₁₀?

I have **3⅓**.

Who has the mixed
number for ¹⁵⁄₇?

I have **2³⁄₁₀**.

Who has the mixed
number for ²⁷⁄₈?

I have **2⅐**.

Who has the mixed
number for ⁹⁄₂?

I have **3⅜**.

Who has the mixed
number for ²⁹⁄₉?

I Have, Who Has!: Math • 5–6 © 2006 Creative Teaching Press

Changing Improper Fractions to Mixed Numbers

I have **3²⁄₉.**

Who has the mixed number for ¹⁹⁄₅?

I have **5¹⁄₆.**

Who has the mixed number for ⁴⁵⁄₁₁?

I have **3⁴⁄₅.**

Who has the mixed number for ¹³⁄₂?

I have **4¹⁄₁₁.**

Who has the mixed number for ¹⁴⁹⁄₁₂?

I have **6½.**

Who has the mixed number for ¹⁵⁄₄?

I have **12⁵⁄₁₂.**

Who has the mixed number for ⁶⁷⁄₁₀?

I have **3¾.**

Who has the mixed number for ²⁶⁄₅?

I have **6⁷⁄₁₀.**

Who has the mixed number for ¹⁰⁰⁄₉?

I have **5¹⁄₅.**

Who has the mixed number for ³¹⁄₆?

I have **11¹⁄₉.**

Who has the mixed number for ⁶²⁄₅?

Changing Improper Fractions to Mixed Numbers

I have **12²/₅**.

Who has the mixed number for ¹¹/₂?

I have **8¼**.

Who has the mixed number for ⁵³/₆?

I have **5½**.

Who has the mixed number for ³⁷/₇?

I have **8⁵/₆**.

Who has the mixed number for ⁷¹/₁₀?

I have **5²/₇**.

Who has the mixed number for ³⁵/₁₁?

I have **7¹/₁₀**.

Who has the mixed number for ⁵⁷/₅?

I have **3²/₁₁**.

Who has the mixed number for ³⁷/₃?

I have **11²/₅**.

Who has the mixed number for ¹⁷/₈?

I have **12⅓**.

Who has the mixed number for ³³/₄?

I have **2⅛**.

Who has the mixed number for ³⁷/₉?

I Have, Who Has?: Math • 5–6 © 2006 Creative Teaching Press

Changing Improper Fractions
to Mixed Numbers

I have **4¹/₉.**

Who has the mixed
number for ³⁷/₁₂?

I have **2¹/₁₅.**

Who has the mixed
number for ⁵⁶/₂₅?

I have **3¹/₁₂.**

Who has the mixed
number for ³¹/₃?

I have **2⁶/₂₅.**

Who has the mixed
number for ²¹⁷/₅₀?

I have **10¹/₃.**

Who has the mixed
number for ⁵¹/₇?

I have **4¹⁷/₅₀.**

Who has the mixed
number for ⁷/₂?

I have **7²/₇.**

Who has the mixed
number for ²⁵/₈?

I have **3½.**

Who has the mixed
number for ⁸⁹/₁₁?

I have **3¹/₈.**

Who has the mixed
number for ³¹/₁₅?

I have **8¹/₁₁.**

Who has the first card?

I Have, Who Has?: Math • 5–6 © 2006 Creative Teaching Press

Changing Improper Fractions to Mixed Numbers

Directions: Follow the path by highlighting the answers as your classmates identify them.

$8\frac{1}{11}$	$8\frac{5}{6}$	$3\frac{2}{9}$	$3\frac{4}{5}$	$2\frac{1}{8}$	$4\frac{17}{50}$	$3\frac{1}{2}$	$8\frac{1}{11}$	**FINISH** ✪
$2\frac{1}{2}$	$10\frac{1}{3}$	$3\frac{3}{8}$	$6\frac{1}{2}$	$7\frac{2}{3}$	$2\frac{6}{25}$	$12\frac{1}{3}$	$10\frac{1}{3}$	$3\frac{1}{2}$
$2\frac{1}{7}$	$4\frac{1}{2}$	$2\frac{3}{10}$	$3\frac{3}{4}$	$9\frac{2}{7}$	$2\frac{1}{15}$	$3\frac{1}{8}$	$7\frac{2}{7}$	$10\frac{1}{3}$
$3\frac{1}{3}$	$2\frac{1}{5}$	$2\frac{1}{6}$	$5\frac{1}{5}$	$6\frac{2}{5}$	$3\frac{1}{2}$	$2\frac{1}{5}$	$4\frac{1}{9}$	$3\frac{1}{12}$
$2\frac{1}{2}$	$6\frac{1}{4}$	$4\frac{2}{3}$	$5\frac{1}{6}$	$3\frac{4}{5}$	$3\frac{2}{11}$	$12\frac{1}{3}$	$2\frac{1}{8}$	$8\frac{1}{12}$
$3\frac{1}{5}$	$7\frac{1}{11}$	$12\frac{5}{12}$	$4\frac{1}{11}$	$7\frac{3}{4}$	$5\frac{2}{7}$	$8\frac{1}{4}$	$11\frac{2}{5}$	$5\frac{1}{5}$
START ✪	$8\frac{1}{6}$	$6\frac{7}{10}$	$11\frac{1}{9}$	$12\frac{2}{5}$	$5\frac{1}{2}$	$8\frac{5}{6}$	$7\frac{1}{10}$	$4\frac{1}{2}$

Choose 15 of the mixed numbers that are **not** highlighted in the table above. Rewrite them as improper fractions.

1. _____

2. _____

3. _____

4. _____

5. _____

6. _____

7. _____

8. _____

9. _____

10. _____

11. _____

12. _____

13. _____

14. _____

15. _____

I Have, Who Has?: Math • 5–6 © 2006 Creative Teaching Press

Changing Mixed Numbers
to Improper Fractions

I have the **first card.**

Who has the improper
fraction for 2½?

I have ⁸/₅.

Who has the improper
fraction for 2⅑?

I have ⁵/₂.

Who has the improper
fraction for 5⅔?

I have ¹⁹/₉.

Who has the improper
fraction for 2⅚?

I have ¹⁷/₃.

Who has the improper
fraction for 3⅖?

I have ¹⁷/₆.

Who has the improper
fraction for 1⅘?

I have ¹⁷/₅.

Who has the improper
fraction for 6⅔?

I have ⁹/₅.

Who has the improper
fraction for 2³/₇?

I have ²⁰/₃.

Who has the improper
fraction for 1³/₅?

I have ¹⁷/₇.

Who has the improper
fraction for 1²/₉?

I Have, Who Has? Math • 5–6 © 2006 Creative Teaching Press

Changing Mixed Numbers to Improper Fractions

I have $^{11}/_9$.

Who has the improper fraction for $4\frac{1}{2}$?

I have $^{15}/_7$.

Who has the improper fraction for $8\frac{3}{8}$?

I have $^9/_2$.

Who has the improper fraction for $3\frac{2}{11}$?

I have $^6/_8$.

Who has the improper fraction for $9\frac{4}{5}$?

I have $^{35}/_{11}$.

Who has the improper fraction for $2\frac{5}{12}$?

I have $^{49}/_5$.

Who has the improper fraction for $6\frac{2}{5}$?

I have $^{29}/_{12}$.

Who has the improper fraction for $3\frac{1}{4}$?

I have $^{32}/_5$.

Who has the improper fraction for $10\frac{2}{3}$?

I have $^{13}/_4$.

Who has the improper fraction for $2\frac{1}{7}$?

I have $^{32}/_3$.

Who has the improper fraction for $6\frac{1}{3}$?

I Have, Who Has?: Math • 5–6 © 2006 Creative Teaching Press

Changing Mixed Numbers to Improper Fractions

I have $19/3$.

Who has the improper fraction for $5\frac{3}{5}$?

I have $38/9$.

Who has the improper fraction for $11\frac{1}{3}$?

I have $28/5$.

Who has the improper fraction for $6\frac{1}{7}$?

I have $34/3$.

Who has the improper fraction for $2\frac{4}{25}$?

I have $43/7$.

Who has the improper fraction for $5\frac{3}{4}$?

I have $54/25$.

Who has the improper fraction for $11\frac{1}{2}$?

I have $23/4$.

Who has the improper fraction for $7\frac{1}{5}$?

I have $23/2$.

Who has the improper fraction for $3\frac{9}{10}$?

I have $36/5$.

Who has the improper fraction for $4\frac{2}{9}$?

I have $39/10$.

Who has the improper fraction for $12\frac{1}{2}$?

Changing Mixed Numbers
to Improper Fractions

I have ²⁵/₁₂.

Who has the improper
fraction for 3²/₂₅?

I have ⁷¹/₁₀.

Who has the improper
fraction for 9²/₃?

I have ⁷⁷/₅.

Who has the improper
fraction for 12⅓?

I have ²⁹/₃.

Who has the improper
fraction for 3⁴/₂₅?

I have ³⁷/₃.

Who has the improper
fraction for 2⁵/₆?

I have ⁷⁹/₂₅.

Who has the improper
fraction for 1¾?

I have ¹⁷/₆.

Who has the improper
fraction for 5³/₁₁?

I have ⁷/₄.

Who has the improper
fraction for 5¹/₁₀?

I have ⁵⁸/₁₁.

Who has the improper
fraction for 7¹/₁₀?

I have ⁵¹/₁₀.

Who has the first card?

Changing Mixed Numbers to Improper Fractions

Directions: Follow the path by highlighting the answers as your classmates identify them.

$17/3$	$28/5$	$43/7$	$27/2$	$23/2$	$39/10$	$7/4$	**FINISH** ✪
$22/5$	$19/3$	$23/4$	$90/8$	$54/25$	$25/12$	$79/25$	$51/10$
$32/5$	$32/3$	$36/5$	$38/9$	$34/3$	$77/5$	$29/3$	$71/10$
$49/5$	$57/5$	$42/5$	$91/9$	$52/7$	$37/3$	$17/6$	$58/11$
$67/8$	$15/7$	$80/25$	$9/2$	$11/9$	$80/7$	$20/3$	$17/5$
$15/2$	$13/4$	$29/12$	$35/11$	$17/7$	$25/4$	$8/5$	$17/3$
$26/3$	$16/3$	$100/12$	$61/6$	$9/5$	$17/6$	$19/9$	$5/2$
$55/4$	$31/5$	$99/10$	$16/3$	$59/5$	$19/5$	$77/12$	**START** ✪

Choose 15 of the improper fractions that are **not** highlighted in the table above. Rewrite them as mixed numbers.

1. _____

2. _____

3. _____

4. _____

5. _____

6. _____

7. _____

8. _____

9. _____

10. _____

11. _____

12. _____

13. _____

14. _____

15. _____

Changing Decimals to Percents

I have the **first card.**

Who has the percent equivalent for forty hundredths (0.40)?

I have **51%.**

Who has the percent equivalent for nine hundredths (0.09)?

I have **40%.**

Who has the percent equivalent for twenty-six hundredths (0.26)?

I have **9%.**

Who has the percent equivalent for five hundredths (0.05)?

I have **26%.**

Who has the percent equivalent for ninety-five hundredths (0.95)?

I have **5%.**

Who has the percent equivalent for six hundredths (0.06)?

I have **95%.**

Who has the percent equivalent for seventy-two hundredths (0.72)?

I have **6%.**

Who has the percent equivalent for twenty-nine hundredths (0.29)?

I have **72%.**

Who has the percent equivalent for fifty-one hundredths (0.51)?

I have **29%.**

Who has the percent equivalent for five tenths (0.5)?

I Have, Who Has?: Math • 5–6 © 2006 Creative Teaching Press

I have **50%**.

Who has the percent equivalent for twenty-one hundredths (0.21)?

I have **16%**.

Who has the percent equivalent for sixty-three hundredths (0.63)?

I have **21%**.

Who has the percent equivalent for ninety-nine hundredths (0.99)?

I have **63%**.

Who has the percent equivalent for seven hundredths (0.07)?

I have **99%**.

Who has the percent equivalent for two tenths (0.2)?

I have 7%.

Who has the percent equivalent for sixty-four hundredths (0.64)?

I have **20%**.

Who has the percent equivalent for eight hundredths (0.08)?

I have **64%**.

Who has the percent equivalent for forty-seven hundredths (0.47)?

I have **8%**.

Who has the percent equivalent for sixteen hundredths (0.16)?

I have **47%**.

Who has the percent equivalent for eighty-four hundredths (0.84)?

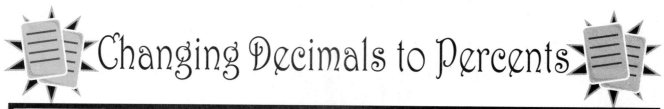

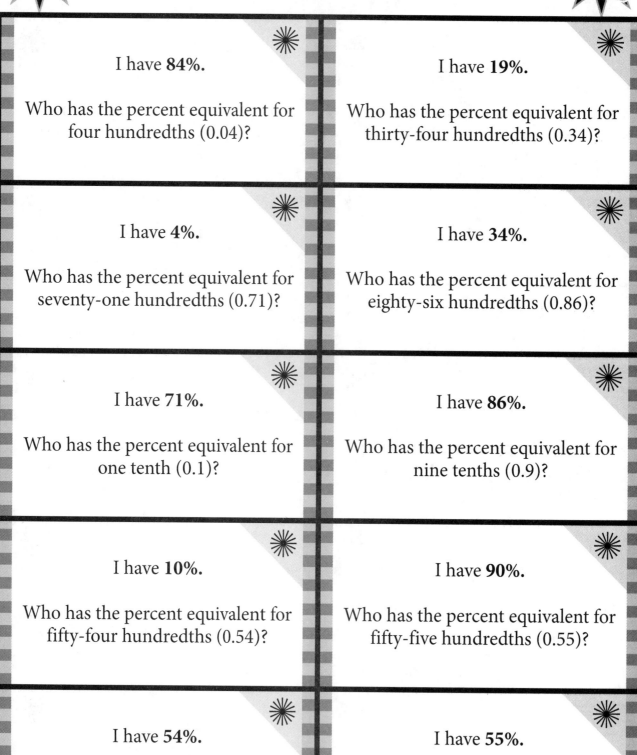

I have **84%**.

Who has the percent equivalent for four hundredths (0.04)?

I have **19%**.

Who has the percent equivalent for thirty-four hundredths (0.34)?

I have **4%**.

Who has the percent equivalent for seventy-one hundredths (0.71)?

I have **34%**.

Who has the percent equivalent for eighty-six hundredths (0.86)?

I have **71%**.

Who has the percent equivalent for one tenth (0.1)?

I have **86%**.

Who has the percent equivalent for nine tenths (0.9)?

I have **10%**.

Who has the percent equivalent for fifty-four hundredths (0.54)?

I have **90%**.

Who has the percent equivalent for fifty-five hundredths (0.55)?

I have **54%**.

Who has the percent equivalent for nineteen hundredths (0.19)?

I have **55%**.

Who has the percent equivalent for sixty-two hundredths (0.62)?

I Have, Who Has?: Math • 5–6 © 2006 Creative Teaching Press

Changing Decimals to Percents

I have **62%**.

Who has the percent equivalent for seventy-nine hundredths (0.79)?

I have **87%**.

Who has the percent equivalent for seventy-three hundredths (0.73)?

I have **79%**.

Who has the percent equivalent for eighty-three hundredths (0.83)?

I have **73%**.

Who has the percent equivalent for twenty-eight hundredths (0.28)?

I have **83%**.

Who has the percent equivalent for thirty-eight hundredths (0.38)?

I have **28%**.

Who has the percent equivalent for eleven hundredths (0.11)?

I have **38%**.

Who has the percent equivalent for one hundredth (0.01)?

I have **11%**.

Who has the percent equivalent for ninety-one hundredths (0.91)?

I have **1%**.

Who has the percent equivalent for eighty-seven hundredths (0.87)?

I have **91%**.

Who has the first card?

Changing Decimals to Percents

Directions: As your classmates identify the answers, draw a line to each number to complete the maze.

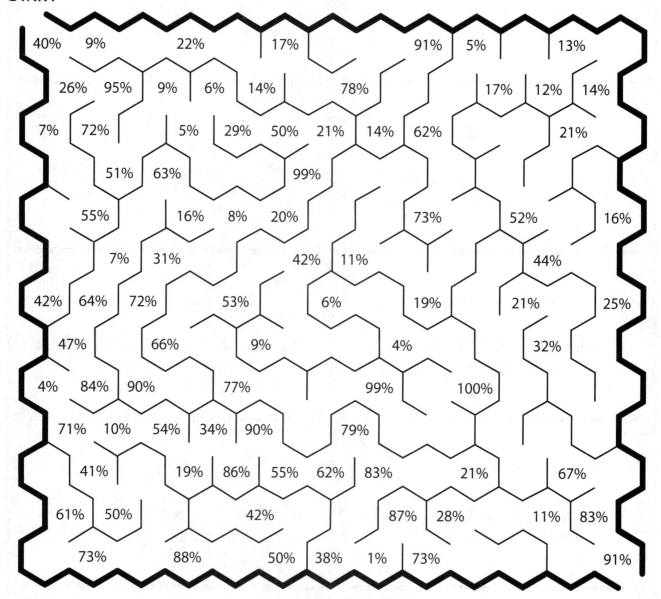

I Have, Who Has?: Math • 5–6 © 2006 Creative Teaching Press

I have the **first card.**

Who has the decimal for 26%?

I have **seventeen hundredths** (0.17).

Who has the decimal for 7%?

I have **twenty-six hundredths** (0.26).

Who has the decimal for 91%?

I have **seven hundredths** (0.07).

Who has the decimal for 76%?

I have **ninety-one hundredths** (0.91).

Who has the decimal for 3%?

I have **seventy-six hundredths** (0.76).

Who has the decimal for 1%?

I have **three hundredths** (0.03).

Who has the decimal for 51%?

I have **one hundredth** (0.01).

Who has the decimal for 58%?

I have **fifty-one hundredths** (0.51).

Who has the decimal for 17%?

I have **fifty-eight hundredths** (0.58).

Who has the decimal for 81%?

I have **eighty-one hundredths** (0.81).

Who has the decimal for 60%?

I have **forty-five hundredths** (0.45).

Who has the decimal for 72%?

I have **six tenths** (0.6).

Who has the decimal for 8%?

I have **seventy-two hundredths** (0.72).

Who has the decimal for 20%?

I have **eight hundredths** (0.08).

Who has the decimal for 90%?

I have **two tenths** (0.2).

Who has the decimal for 4%?

I have **nine tenths** (0.9).

Who has the decimal for 10%?

I have **four hundredths** (0.04).

Who has the decimal for 70%?

I have **one tenth** (0.1).

Who has the decimal for 45%?

I have **seven tenths** (0.7).

Who has the decimal for 5%?

Changing Percents to Decimals

I have **five hundredths** (0.05).

Who has the decimal for 6%?

I have **twenty-nine hundredths** (0.29).

Who has the decimal for 43%?

I have **six hundredths** (0.06).

Who has the decimal for 50%?

I have **forty-three hundredths** (0.43).

Who has the decimal for one hundred percent (100%)?

I have **five tenths** (0.5).

Who has the decimal for 15%?

I have **one whole** (1.00).

Who has the decimal for 13%?

I have **fifteen hundredths** (0.15).

Who has the decimal for 56%?

I have **thirteen hundredths** (0.13).

Who has the decimal for 63%?

I have **fifty-six hundredths** (0.56).

Who has the decimal for 29%?

I have **sixty-three hundredths** (0.63).

Who has the decimal for 80%?

I Have, Who Has?: Math • 5–6 © 2006 Creative Teaching Press

Changing Percents to Decimals

I have **eight tenths** (0.8).

Who has the decimal for 96%?

I have **seventy-one hundredths** (0.71).

Who has the decimal for 88%?

I have **ninety-six hundredths** (0.96).

Who has the decimal for 2%?

I have **eighty-eight hundredths** (0.88).

Who has the decimal for 9%?

I have **two hundredths** (0.02).

Who has the decimal for 99%?

I have **nine hundredths** (0.09).

Who has the decimal for 30%?

I have **ninety-nine hundredths** (0.99).

Who has the decimal for 40%?

I have **three tenths** (0.3).

Who has the decimal for 24%?

I have **four tenths** (0.4).

Who has the decimal for 71%?

I have **twenty-four hundredths** (0.24).

Who has the first card?

I Have, Who Has?: Math • 5–6 © 2006 Creative Teaching Press

Changing Percents to Decimals

Directions: Highlight each decimal equivalent in the table below as your classmates identify it.

0.01	0.02	0.03	0.04	0.05	0.06	0.07	0.08	0.09	0.10
0.11	0.12	0.13	0.14	0.15	0.16	0.17	0.18	0.19	0.20
0.21	0.22	0.23	0.24	0.25	0.26	0.27	0.28	0.29	0.30
0.31	0.32	0.33	0.34	0.35	0.36	0.37	0.38	0.39	0.40
0.41	0.42	0.43	0.44	0.45	0.46	0.47	0.48	0.49	0.50
0.51	0.52	0.53	0.54	0.55	0.56	0.57	0.58	0.59	0.60
0.61	0.62	0.63	0.64	0.65	0.66	0.67	0.68	0.69	0.70
0.71	0.72	0.73	0.74	0.75	0.76	0.77	0.78	0.79	0.80
0.81	0.82	0.83	0.84	0.85	0.86	0.87	0.88	0.89	0.90
0.91	0.92	0.93	0.94	0.95	0.96	0.97	0.98	0.99	1.00

Now find pairs of decimals from the chart that are **not** highlighted that will add up to equal 100%. Record the decimals and percents. The first one has been done for you.

1. __0.11__ + __0.89__ = __11__ % + __89__ % = 100%

2. _____ + _____ = _____ % + _____ % = 100%

3. _____ + _____ = _____ % + _____ % = 100%

4. _____ + _____ = _____ % + _____ % = 100%

5. _____ + _____ = _____ % + _____ % = 100%

6. _____ + _____ = _____ % + _____ % = 100%

7. _____ + _____ = _____ % + _____ % = 100%

8. _____ + _____ = _____ % + _____ % = 100%

9. _____ + _____ = _____ % + _____ % = 100%

10. _____ + _____ = _____ % + _____ % = 100%

11. _____ + _____ = _____ % + _____ % = 100%

12. _____ + _____ = _____ % + _____ % = 100%

I Have, Who Has?: Math • 5–6 © 2006 Creative Teaching Press

I have the **first card.**

Who has a ratio for 86%?

I have **7:10.**

Who has a ratio for 9%?

I have **86:100.**

Who has a ratio for 61%?

I have **9:100.**

Who has a ratio for 53%?

I have **61:100.**

Who has a ratio for 3%?

I have **53:100.**

Who has a ratio for 21%?

I have **3:100.**

Who has a ratio for 59%?

I have **21:100.**

Who has a ratio for 10%?

I have **59:100.**

Who has a ratio for 70%?

I have **1:10.**

Who has a ratio for 75%?

Changing Percents to Ratios

I have **3:4.**

Who has a ratio for 8%?

I have **81:100.**

Who has a ratio for 90%?

I have **8:100.**

Who has a ratio for 25%?

I have **9:10.**

Who has a ratio for 5%?

I have **1:4.**

Who has a ratio for 34%?

I have **5:100.**

Who has a ratio for 88%?

I have **34:100.**

Who has a ratio for 97%?

I have **88:100.**

Who has a ratio for 60%?

I have **97:100.**

Who has a ratio for 81%?

I have **3:5.**

Who has a ratio for 24%?

Changing Percents to Ratios

I have **24:100**.

Who has a ratio for 40%?

I have **29:100**.

Who has a ratio for 35%?

I have **2:5**.

Who has a ratio for 92%?

I have **35:100**.

Who has a ratio for 39%?

I have **92:100**.

Who has a ratio for 50%?

I have **39:100**.

Who has a ratio for 2%?

I have **1:2**.

Who has a ratio for 80%?

I have **2:100**.

Who has a ratio for 1%?

I have **4:5**.

Who has a ratio for 29%?

I have **1:100**.

Who has a ratio for 95%?

I have **95:100.**

Who has a ratio for 30%?

I have **62:100.**

Who has a ratio for 68%?

I have **3:10.**

Who has a ratio for 18%?

I have **68:100.**

Who has a ratio for 20%?

I have **18:100.**

Who has a ratio for 7%?

I have **1:5.**

Who has a ratio for 15%?

I have **7:100.**

Who has a ratio for 6%?

I have **15:100.**

Who has a ratio for 91%?

I have **6:100.**

Who has a ratio for 62%?

I have **91:100.**

Who has the first card?

Changing Percents to Ratios

Directions: Follow the path by highlighting the answers as your classmates identify them.

2:100	1:100	95:100	3:10	12:100	50:100	**FINISH** ⭐
39:100	27:100	9:100	18:100	7:100	2:5	91:100
35:100	29:100	4:5	1:10	6:100	62:100	15:100
14:100	23:100	1:2	92:100	29:100	68:100	1:5
59:100	7:10	81:100	2:5	24:100	8:10	21:100
3:100	9:100	53:100	17:100	3:5	88:100	83:100
61:100	19:100	21:100	8:100	1:4	5:100	71:100
86:100	3:5	1:10	3:4	34:100	9:10	22:100
START ⭐	49:100	1:2	7:10	97:100	81:100	3:4

Choose ten ratios from above that are **not** highlighted. List them. Then change them to percents. The first one has been done for you.

1. ___49___ : ___100___ = ___49___ %

2. _____ : _____ = _____ %

3. _____ : _____ = _____ %

4. _____ : _____ = _____ %

5. _____ : _____ = _____ %

6. _____ : _____ = _____ %

7. _____ : _____ = _____ %

8. _____ : _____ = _____ %

9. _____ : _____ = _____ %

10. _____ : _____ = _____ %

I Have, Who Has?: Math • 5–6 © 2006 Creative Teaching Press

Changing Ratios to Percents

I have the **first card.** Who has the percent equivalent for the ratio of 65:100?	I have **49%.** Who has the percent equivalent for the ratio of 22:100?
I have **65%.** Who has the percent equivalent for the ratio of 3:100?	I have **22%.** Who has the percent equivalent for the ratio of 57:100?
I have **3%.** Who has the percent equivalent for the ratio of 1:4?	I have **57%.** Who has the percent equivalent for the ratio of 9:100?
I have **25%.** Who has the percent equivalent for the ratio of 12:100?	I have **9%.** Who has the percent equivalent for the ratio of 3:5?
I have **12%.** Who has the percent equivalent for the ratio of 49:100?	I have **60%.** Who has the percent equivalent for the ratio of 96:100?

Changing Ratios to Percents

I have **96%.**

Who has the percent equivalent
for the ratio of 54:100?

I have **30%.**

Who has the percent equivalent
for the ratio of 23:100?

I have **54%.**

Who has the percent equivalent
for the ratio of 79:100?

I have **23%.**

Who has the percent equivalent
for the ratio of 1:1?

I have **79%.**

Who has the percent equivalent
for the ratio of 44:100?

I have **100%.**

Who has the percent equivalent
for the ratio of 6:100?

I have **44%.**

Who has the percent equivalent
for the ratio of 61:100?

I have **6%.**

Who has the percent equivalent
for the ratio of 3:4?

I have **61%.**

Who has the percent equivalent
for the ratio of 3:10?

I have **75%.**

Who has the percent equivalent
for the ratio of 77:100?

I Have, Who Has?: Math • 5–6 © 2006 Creative Teaching Press

Changing Ratios to Percents

I have **77%**.

Who has the percent equivalent
for the ratio of 26:100?

I have **29%**.

Who has the percent equivalent
for the ratio of 86:100?

I have **26%**.

Who has the percent equivalent
for the ratio of 58:100?

I have **86%**.

Who has the percent equivalent
for the ratio of 42:100?

I have **58%**.

Who has the percent equivalent
for the ratio of 7:10?

I have **42%**.

Who has the percent equivalent
for the ratio of 2:5?

I have **70%**.

Who has the percent equivalent
for the ratio of 47:100?

I have **40%**.

Who has the percent equivalent
for the ratio of 72:100?

I have **47%**.

Who has the percent equivalent
for the ratio of 29:100?

I have **72%**.

Who has the percent equivalent
for the ratio of 9:10?

 # Changing Ratios to Percents

I have **90%.**

Who has the percent equivalent for the ratio of 17:100?

I have **39%.**

Who has the percent equivalent for the ratio of 1:100?

I have **17%.**

Who has the percent equivalent for the ratio of 69:100?

I have **1%.**

Who has the percent equivalent for the ratio of 1:2?

I have **69%.**

Who has the percent equivalent for the ratio of 4:5?

I have **50%.**

Who has the percent equivalent for the ratio of 74:100?

I have **80%.**

Who has the percent equivalent for the ratio of 36:100?

I have **74%.**

Who has the percent equivalent for the ratio of 1:5?

I have **36%.**

Who has the percent equivalent for the ratio of 39:100?

I have **20%.**

Who has the first card?

I Have, Who Has?: Math • 5–6 © 2006 Creative Teaching Press

Changing Ratios to Percents

Directions: Highlight the percentages in the table as your classmates identify them.

1%	2%	3%	4%	5%	6%	7%	8%	9%	10%
11%	12%	13%	14%	15%	16%	17%	18%	19%	20%
21%	22%	23%	24%	25%	26%	27%	28%	29%	30%
31%	32%	33%	34%	35%	36%	37%	38%	39%	40%
41%	42%	43%	44%	45%	46%	47%	48%	49%	50%
51%	52%	53%	54%	55%	56%	57%	58%	59%	60%
61%	62%	63%	64%	65%	66%	67%	68%	69%	70%
71%	72%	73%	74%	75%	76%	77%	78%	79%	80%
81%	82%	83%	84%	85%	86%	87%	88%	89%	90%
91%	92%	93%	94%	95%	96%	97%	98%	99%	100%

Choose ten percentages from the table above that you did **not** highlight. Write a ratio for each percentage.

1. _____ % = _____ : _____

2. _____ % = _____ : _____

3. _____ % = _____ : _____

4. _____ % = _____ : _____

5. _____ % = _____ : _____

6. _____ % = _____ : _____

7. _____ % = _____ : _____

8. _____ % = _____ : _____

9. _____ % = _____ : _____

10. _____ % = _____ : _____

Comparing Integers

I have the first card. Who has the greater of these two integers: ⁻9, 8?	**I have 32.** Who has the lesser of these two integers: ⁻42, ⁻29?
I have 8. Who has the greater of these two integers: ⁻9, ⁻15?	**I have ⁻42.** Who has the greater of these two integers: ⁻33, 16?
I have ⁻9. Who has the lesser of these two integers: ⁻14, 6?	**I have 16.** Who has the lesser of these two integers: ⁻19, ⁻10?
I have ⁻14. Who has the greater of these two integers: ⁻5, 5?	**I have ⁻19.** Who has the greater of these two integers: ⁻99, ⁻87?
I have 5. Who has the lesser of these two integers: 35, 32?	**I have ⁻87.** Who has the lesser of these two integers: 21, 26?

I Have, Who Has?: Math • 5–6 © 2006 Creative Teaching Press

Comparing Integers

I have **21.**

Who has the greater of
these two integers:
-23, -29?

I have **6.**

Who has the lesser of
these two integers:
-10, -14?

I have **-23.**

Who has the greater of
these two integers:
13, -14?

I have **-14.**

Who has the greater of
these two integers:
46, -48?

I have **13.**

Who has the lesser of
these two integers:
-14, -20?

I have **46.**

Who has the lesser of
these two integers:
-2, -5?

I have **-20.**

Who has the lesser of
these two integers:
66, 70?

I have **-5.**

Who has the greater of
these two integers:
35, -62?

I have **66.**

Who has the greater of
these two integers:
6, -9?

I have **35.**

Who has the greater of
these two integers:
-72, -51?

I Have, Who Has?: Math • 5–6 © 2006 Creative Teaching Press

Comparing Integers

I have -**51**.

Who has the lesser of
these two integers:
-9, -10?

I have -**2**.

Who has the greater of
these two integers:
-29, -33?

I have -**10**.

Who has the lesser of
these two integers:
47, 57?

I have -**29**.

Who has the lesser of
these two integers:
-7, -4?

I have **47**.

Who has the greater of
these two integers:
98, -99?

I have -**7**.

Who has the greater of
these two integers:
70, -72?

I have **98**.

Who has the lesser of
these two integers:
29, 26?

I have **70**.

Who has the lesser of
these two integers:
-33, -45?

I have **26**.

Who has the greater of
these two integers:
-7, -2?

I have -**45**.

Who has the greater of
these two integers:
-48, -52?

I Have, Who Has?: Math • 5–6 © 2006 Creative Teaching Press

Comparing Integers

I have **⁻48.**

Who has the lesser of
these two integers:
59, ⁻62?

I have **4.**

Who has the lesser of
these two integers:
⁻37, ⁻33?

I have **⁻62.**

Who has the greater of
these two integers:
⁻33, ⁻45?

I have **⁻37.**

Who has the greater of
these two integers:
⁻66, 57?

I have **⁻33.**

Who has the lesser of
these two integers:
⁻12, 4?

I have **57.**

Who has the greater of
these two integers:
100, ⁻105?

I have **⁻12.**

Who has the greater of
these two integers:
⁻62, ⁻70?

I have **100.**

Who has the lesser of
these two integers:
⁻61, ⁻72?

I have **⁻62.**

Who has the greater of
these two integers:
4, ⁻7?

I have **⁻72.**

Who has the first card?

I Have, Who Has?: Math • 5–6 © 2006 Creative Teaching Press

Comparing Integers

Directions: As your classmates identify the answers, write the integers in the boxes. Start at the top and go from left to right.

4									
3									
2									
1									0
	A	B	C	D	E	F	G	H	I	J

Use the grid coordinates above to write the corresponding number for each coordinate. Then complete each equation.

1. B4 + E2 = _____

2. H2 – B1 = _____

3. A4 + H4 = _____

4. C3 – I1 = _____

5. D2 – G2 = _____

6. A2 + D3 = _____

7. H2 – I3 = _____

8. F4 – G1 = _____

9. J4 + J3 = _____

10. B3 – C4 = _____

11. G2 + E3 = _____

12. A4 – C1 = _____

13. E2 + H1 = _____

14. D4 + H3 = _____

15. F2 – A3 = _____

I Have, Who Has?: Math • 5–6 © 2006 Creative Teaching Press

Math Terminology

I have the **first card**.

Who has the word that describes the space inside an object?

I have **positive numbers**.

Who has the word for the number that goes under the bar in a fraction?

I have **area**.

Who has the word that describes the distance around an object?

I have **denominator**.

Who has the word for the answer to a multiplication problem?

I have **perimeter**.

Who has the words that mean a whole number that has more than two factors?

I have **product**.

Who has the words that mean all of the numbers less than zero?

I have **composite number**.

Who has the word for the answer to a division problem?

I have **negative numbers**.

Who has the word for a number close to an exact amount?

I have **quotient**.

Who has the words for all of the numbers that are greater than zero?

I have **estimate**.

Who has the words that describe the distance of a number from zero on a number line?

Math Terminology

I have absolute value.

Who has the word for the top number in a fraction?

I have mean.

Who has the words that mean the smallest number that is a multiple of two or more numbers?

I have numerator.

Who has the words for the sum of the area of all surfaces?

I have least common multiple or LCM.

Who has the words for a number represented by a whole number and a fraction?

I have surface area.

Who has the name for the largest whole number that is a common factor of two or more numbers?

I have mixed number.

Who has the word that names the answer to a subtraction problem?

I have greatest common factor or GCF.

Who has the word that describes what two lines do when they meet or cross at a common point?

I have difference.

Who has the words that name a whole number that cannot be divided by any number other than itself and one?

I have intersect.

Who has the word that means the average of a set of numbers in which you add all the numbers together and divide them by the number of numbers?

I have prime number.

Who has the word for the ratio of a number to 100?

I Have, Who Has?: Math • 5–6 © 2006 Creative Teaching Press

Math Terminology

I have **percent.**

Who has the word that means the number that appears the most often in a set of numbers?

I have **improper fraction.**

Who has the word that describes fractions that have the same value?

I have **mode.**

Who has the word that describes the amount a container can hold?

I have **equivalent.**

Who has the word that names the graph that uses bars to display data based on how frequently it occurs within equal intervals?

I have **capacity.**

Who has the word that names the set of whole numbers that are positive and negative?

I have **histogram.**

Who has the word for the likelihood that an event will happen?

I have **integers.**

Who has the word that describes figures that have the same size and shape?

I have **probability.**

Who has the word that shows a comparison of two numbers by division?

I have **congruent.**

Who has the words that name the type of fraction in which the numerator is larger than the denominator?

I have **ratio.**

Who has the word for the number that is to be divided in a division problem?

I Have, Who Has?: Math • 5–6 © 2006 Creative Teaching Press

Math Terminology

I have **dividend.**

Who has the word for an algebraic or numerical sentence that shows that two quantities are equal?

I have **Venn diagram.**

Who has the words for a way to write numbers by showing the value of each digit?

I have **equation.**

Who has the word for a number that is multiplied by another number to find a product?

I have **expanded form.**

Who has the word for a number that names a part of a whole or a part of a group?

I have **factor.**

Who has the word for a number that shows how many times the base is used as a factor?

I have **fraction.**

Who has the word for a metric unit for measuring temperature?

I have **exponent.**

Who has the word for the difference between the greatest number and the least number in a set of data?

I have **degrees Celsius.**

Who has the name for a customary unit for measuring temperature?

I have **range.**

Who has the word for a diagram that shows the relationships among sets of things?

I have **degrees Fahrenheit.**

Who has the first card?

I Have, Who Has?: Math • 5–6 © 2006 Creative Teaching Press

Math Terminology

Directions: Follow the path by highlighting the math terms as your classmates identify them.

START ✪	area	Venn diagram	expanded form	fraction	measurement	FINISH ✪
mass	perimeter	division	range	geometry	degrees Celsius	degrees Fahrenheit
composite number	volume	addition	formula	exponent	factor	equation
quotient	number line	absolute value	numerator	probability	ratio	dividend
positive number	denominator	estimate	surface area	histogram	square number	algebra
bar graph	product	negative numbers	greatest common factor or GCF	line graph	equivalent	multiplication
circle graph	least common multiple or LCM	mean	intersect	mode	capacity	improper fraction
mixed number	difference	prime number	percent	decimal	integers	congruent

Choose five highlighted words from the table above. Write a definition for each word.

1. _____ = _____

2. _____ = _____

3. _____ = _____

4. _____ = _____

5. _____ = _____

Extreme Mental Math

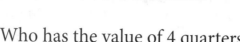

I have the **first card.**

Who has the value of 4 quarters • minus the number of ounces in a pound • divided by 7 • times 3?

I have **96.**

Who has the number of sides on a hexagon • multiplied by 8 • plus 2 • divided by the value of a nickel?

I have **36.**

Who has two dozen • divided by a half dozen • raised to the power of two • divided by 8 • times 15?

I have **10.**

Who has five dozen • divided by 6 • times 4 • plus the number of inches in a foot • minus 2 • doubled • minus 1?

I have **30.**

Who has the value of 6 dimes • divided by 10 • times 9 • minus 20 • plus a half dozen • divided by 10 • multiplied by 11?

I have **99.**

Who has the number of centimeters in a meter • divided by 5 • times the number of feet in a yard • minus the value of a quarter • divided by 5 • times the number of cups in a pint?

I have **44.**

Who has the value of 3 dimes and a nickel • doubled • plus the number of hours in a day • plus the square root of 36 • divided by 25?

I have **14.**

Who has the number of weeks in a year • subtract 2 • doubled • divided by 10 • times 9?

I have **4.**

Who has the number of quarters in a dollar • times 10 • divided by the number of sides on a pentagon • multiplied by a dozen?

I have **90.**

Who has the number of inches in a yard • divided by 3 • times 4 • plus 20 • minus 3?

I Have, Who Has?: Math • 5–6 © 2006 Creative Teaching Press

I have **65.**

Who has the number of hours in a day • doubled • divided by 4 • times 6 • plus 3 • divided by the value of a quarter?

I have **56.**

Who has four squared • minus 1 • doubled • plus the value of a dime • minus 20?

I have **3.**

Who has the number of ounces in a pound • plus 4 • times 5?

I have **20.**

Who has the square root of 144 • times 3 • divided by 9 • times the value of a quarter • split in half?

I have **100.**

Who has six dozen • minus 2 • divided by 7 • times the number of sides on a triangle • plus 2?

I have **50.**

Who has 3 raised to the third power • minus 2 • times 3 • plus 5 • plus 8?

I have **32.**

Who has the perimeter of a square with a side of 10 inches • divided by 4 • times 8 • plus 1?

I have **88.**

Who has the square root of 121 • times 6 • plus 4 • divided by 10?

I have **81.**

Who has the value of 5 nickels • doubled • divided by 10 • times 11 • plus 1?

I have **7.**

Who has the number of minutes in an hour • minus 10 • times 2 • plus 7?

I Have, Who Has? Math • 5–6 © 2006 Creative Teaching Press

Extreme Mental Math

I have 107.

Who has 9 squared • plus 4 • plus the value of a dime • plus the number of pints in a quart?

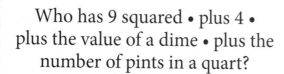
I have 85.

Who has 7 squared • minus 4 • divided by 5 • times the number of cups in a pint?

I have 97.

Who has the number of deciliters in a liter • times 4 • plus 5 • divided by 9 • times the number of days in a week?

I have 18.

Who has the square root of 121 • times 4 • minus 20 • doubled • minus 2?

I have 35.

Who has the square root of 100 • times 9 • minus 20 • plus the number of months in a year • minus 2 • divided by 10?

I have 46.

Who has nine dozen • minus the value of a half-dollar • minus 3 • divided by 11 • times 6 • plus 1?

I have 8.

Who has the number of days in a year • minus the number of cents in $3.00 • plus 10 • minus 60?

I have 31.

Who has the perimeter of a rectangle with sides of 5 by 2 • divided in half • squared?

I have 15.

Who has the area of a rectangle that is 3 by 11 • doubled • minus 1 • plus 20?

I have 49.

Who has the number of dimes in a dollar • times 7 • minus 40 • plus 3 • divided by 11 • squared?

I Have, Who Has?: Math • 5–6 © 2006 Creative Teaching Press

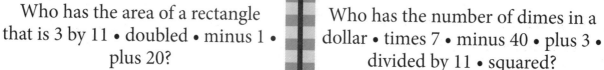

Extreme Mental Math

I have 9.

Who has the number of inches in a yard • divided by 12 • squared • times 10 • plus 2?

I have 60.

Who has the number of degrees in a right angle • split in half • minus 5 • divided by 10 • squared?

I have 92.

Who has the number of years in a decade • squared • divided by the value of a quarter • times a dozen?

I have 16.

Who has the number of weeks in a year • plus 3 • divided by 5 • times a half dozen?

I have 48.

Who has the number of degrees in a right angle • plus 9 • divided by 11 • times 4?

I have 66.

Who has the area of a square with 7-inch sides • minus 5 • divided by 11 • squared • plus 10?

I have 36.

Who has 11 squared • minus the value of 4 quarters • divided by 3 • minus a half dozen • squared • times 5?

I have 26.

Who has the number of sides on an octagon • squared • minus 4 • divided by 5?

I have 5.

Who has the square root of 64 • doubled • minus 1 • times 4?

I have 12.

Who has the first card?

I Have, Who Has?: Math • 5–6 © 2006 Creative Teaching Press

Extreme Mental Math

Directions: As your classmates identify the answers, draw a line to each number to complete the maze.

START

36   5   4   99   14   71   100   32

30   44   96   90   80   3   52

4   10   65   81   56

    23   11   3   43   50

7   21   9   2   19   87   20   5

        8   21   9

6   15   5   68   88   7   97

            77   82   51   92   107   35

21   14   9   8   15

    19   40   41   36   48   49   31   85

35   44   5   60   46   18

            72   43   66   12

71   38   66   59   16   26

FINISH

Write three of your own mental math problems.

1. _____

2. _____

3. _____

Have a partner solve your problems.

I Have, Who Has?: Math • 5–6 © 2006 Creative Teaching Press

Absolute Value and Addition/ Subtraction of Integers

I have the **first card.**

Who has the absolute value of ⁻1?

I have ⁺**72.**

Who has ⁺5 + ⁻9?

I have **1.**

Who has ⁻12 − ⁻10?

I have ⁻**4.**

Who has ⁻7 + ⁻8?

I have ⁻**2.**

Who has ⁻13 + ⁺3?

I have ⁻**15.**

Who has the absolute value of ⁻62?

I have ⁻**10.**

Who has the absolute value of 37?

I have **62.**

Who has ⁺12 − ⁻1?

I have **37.**

Who has ⁺60 + ⁺12?

I have **13.**

Who has ⁻12 + ⁻10?

I Have, Who Has? Math • 5–6 © 2006 Creative Teaching Press

Absolute Value and Addition/ Subtraction of Integers

I have -**22**.

Who has -11 + +10?

I have **12**.

Who has the absolute value of -2?

I have -**1**.

Who has the absolute value of -6?

I have **2**.

Who has +15 – -5?

I have **6**.

Who has the absolute value of 8?

I have +**20**.

Who has +18 – -1?

I have **8**.

Who has -30 – -5?

I have +**19**.

Who has the absolute value of -4?

I have -**25**.

Who has the absolute value of -12?

I have **4**.

Who has +19 – -5?

I have +24.

Who has -7 + +10?

I have +26.

Who has -6 + -2?

I have +3.

Who has -25 + +5?

I have -8.

Who has the absolute value of -21?

I have -20.

Who has the absolute value of 7?

I have 21.

Who has -50 – -50?

I have 7.

Who has -40 + +10?

I have 0.

Who has -10 + -17?

I have -30.

Who has +25 – -1?

I have -27.

Who has the absolute value of -15?

Absolute Value and Addition/ Subtraction of Integers

I have **15.**

Who has the absolute value of ⁻22?

I have **30.**

Who has the absolute value of ⁺25?

I have **22.**

Who has ⁻10 – ⁻5?

I have **25.**

Who has ⁺28 + ⁺3?

I have **⁻5.**

Who has ⁻12 + ⁺5?

I have **31.**

Who has ⁻8 + ⁻9?

I have **⁻7.**

Who has ⁻7 + ⁺12?

I have **⁻17.**

Who has ⁻23 – ⁻10?

I have **⁺5.**

Who has the absolute value of ⁻30?

I have **⁻13.**

Who has the first card?

I Have, Who Has?: Math • 5–6 © 2006 Creative Teaching Press

Absolute Value and Addition/ Subtraction of Integers

Directions: As your classmates identify the answers, write the integers in the boxes. Start at the top and go from left to right.

T	N	V	R	S	E	D	E	U	A
A	R	M	W	E	T	O	L	E	N
M	N	A	M	R	E	E	Y	O	K
									12
I	E	T	C	E	V	S	D	E	T

Now rewrite the integers in each row in order from smallest to largest. Also, rewrite the letter that goes with each integer to reveal four fun ten-letter words.

Number Patterns

I have the first card.

Who has the next number in this pattern: 1, 2, 3, 4?

I have 50.

Who has the next number in this pattern: 3, 5, 7, 9, 11?

I have 5.

Who has the next number in this pattern: 2, 4, 6, 8?

I have 13.

Who has the next number in this pattern: ⁻1, ⁻2, ⁻3, ⁻4?

I have 10.

Who has the next number in this pattern: 3, 6, 9, 12?

I have ⁻5.

Who has the next number in this pattern: ⁻6, ⁻8, ⁻10?

I have 15.

Who has the next number in this pattern: 4, 8, 12, 16?

I have ⁻12.

Who has the next number in this pattern: 1, 2, 4, 8?

I have 20.

Who has the next number in this pattern: 10, 20, 30, 40?

I have 16.

Who has the next number in this pattern: 5, 10, 15, 20?

I Have, Who Has?: Math • 5–6 © 2006 Creative Teaching Press

Number Patterns

I have **25.**

Who has the next number in this pattern: 6, 12, 18?

I have **45.**

Who has the next number in this pattern: 16, 24, 32, 40?

I have **24.**

Who has the next number in this pattern: 1, 4, 9, 16, 25?

I have **48.**

Who has the next number in this pattern: 5, 12, 19, 26?

I have **36.**

Who has the next number in this pattern: 95, 90, 85, 80?

I have **33.**

Who has the next number in this pattern: 100, 200, 300?

I have **75.**

Who has the next number in this pattern: 21, 28, 35, 42?

I have **400.**

Who has the next number in this pattern: 51, 61, 71, 81?

I have **49.**

Who has the next number in this pattern: 9, 18, 27, 36?

I have **91.**

Who has the next number in this pattern: 10, 30, 50, 70?

I Have, Who Has?: Math • 5–6 © 2006 Creative Teaching Press

Number Patterns

I have **90.**

Who has the next number in this pattern: 22, 33, 44?

I have **42.**

Who has the next number in this pattern: 15, 12, 9, 6?

I have **55.**

Who has the next number in this pattern: 24, 36, 48?

I have **3.**

Who has the next number in this pattern: 240, 120, 60?

I have **60.**

Who has the next number in this pattern: 20, 17, 14, 11?

I have **30.**

Who has the next number in this pattern: 3, 9, 27?

I have **8.**

Who has the next number in this pattern: 90, 81, 72, 63?

I have **81.**

Who has the next number in this pattern: 4, 16, 64?

I have **54.**

Who has the next number in this pattern: 58, 54, 50, 46?

I have **256.**

Who has the next number in this pattern: 63, 68, 73, 78?

I Have, Who Has?: Math • 5–6 © 2006 Creative Teaching Press

Number Patterns

I have **83.**

Who has the next number in this pattern: 15, 21, 27, 33?

I have **34.**

Who has the next number in this pattern: 22, 44, 66?

I have **39.**

Who has the next number in this pattern: -15, -13, -11?

I have **88.**

Who has the next number in this pattern: 8, 6, 4?

I have **⁻9.**

Who has the next number in this pattern: 25, 50, 100, 200?

I have **2.**

Who has the next number in this pattern: 15, 30, 60, 120?

I have **400.**

Who has the next number in this pattern: 27, 22, 17, 12?

I have **240.**

Who has the next number in this pattern: 10, 100, 1,000?

I have **7.**

Who has the next number in this pattern: 10, 16, 22, 28?

I have **10,000.**

Who has the first card?

Number Patterns

Directions: Follow the path by highlighting the answers as your classmates identify them.

59	35	⁻12	⁻20	54	42	57	**FINISH** ★
100	⁻5	0	16	8	3	58	10,000
89	13	25	1,000	60	73	30	240
50	⁻4	24	39	21	55	81	2
20	200	29	36	333	90	256	88
44	15	75	243	105	91	83	34
5	10	49	71	400	39	46	7
START ★	67	45	48	33	⁻1	⁻9	400

Create five of your own number patterns. Then have a partner add five more numbers to each of your patterns.

1._____

2._____

3._____

4._____

5._____

I Have, Who Has?: Math • 5–6 © 2006 Creative Teaching Press

Note: Display Evaluating Expressions 1 Overhead Transparency (page 136) during this game.

I have the **first card.**

Who has $10x - 1$?

I have **6.**

Who has $y + 26$?

I have **79.**

Who has $\frac{1}{2}y + 1$?

I have **76.**

Who has $2y - 8$?

I have **26.**

Who has $11x$?

I have **92.**

Who has $3x - 4$?

I have **88.**

Who has $y - 1$?

I have **20.**

Who has $2y - 1$?

I have **49.**

Who has $48 \div x$?

I have **99.**

Who has $x + 5$?

I have **13.**

Who has $y + 3$?

I have **50.**

Who has $y + 36$?

I have **53.**

Who has $6x + 10$?

I have **86.**

Who has $x + 1$?

I have **58.**

Who has $10 - x$?

I have **9.**

Who has $11x + 2$?

I have **2.**

Who has $9x$?

I have **90.**

Who has $20 + x$?

I have **72.**

Who has $2y - 50$?

I have **28.**

Who has $2y - 5$?

I have **95.**

Who has $10x + 1$?

I have **75.**

Who has $6x$?

I have **81.**

Who has $y - 9$?

I have **48.**

Who has $10x + 3$?

I have **41.**

Who has $y + 1$?

I have **83.**

Who has $30 - x$?

I have **51.**

Who has $y \div 10$?

I have **22.**

Who has $12x$?

I have **5.**

Who has $y + \frac{1}{2}y$?

I have **96.**

Who has $5x + 3$?

I have **43.**

Who has $5x + 2$?

I have **29.**

Who has $\frac{1}{2}y$?

I have **42.**

Who has $y + 9$?

I have **25.**

Who has $2x$?

I have **59.**

Who has $2x - 1$?

I have **16.**

Who has $2y - 15$?

I have **15.**

Who has $110 - y$?

I have **85.**

Who has $y + 2$?

I have **60.**

Who has $3x + 5$?

I have **52.**

Who has the first card?

Evaluating Expressions 1

Directions: As your classmates identify the answers to the algebraic equations, write the numbers in the boxes. Start at the top and go from left to right.

x = 8	y = 50

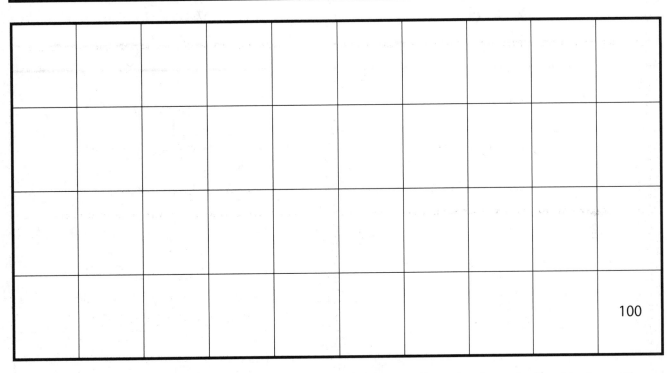

								100

Write an algebraic equation in terms of *x* and *y* for the first and last numbers of each row in the table above. The first one has been done for you.

1. _____ 9*x* + 7 = 79 _____   5. _____

2. _____   6. _____

3. _____   7. _____

4. _____   8. _____

Evaluating Expressions 1 Overhead Transparency

Teacher directions: Copy this page on an overhead transparency. Display the transparency. Cover the entire page with a piece of paper. As a student reads his or her card, show the same equation to help those who need the visual image to solve algebraic equations. They are listed from left to right so you can move the paper below the row.

$x = 8$		$y = 50$	
$10x - 1$	$\frac{1}{2}y + 1$	$11x$	$y - 1$
$48 \div x$	$y + 26$	$2y - 8$	$3x - 4$
$2y - 1$	$x + 5$	$y + 3$	$6x + 10$
$10 - x$	$9x$	$2y - 50$	$y + 36$
$x + 1$	$11x + 2$	$20 + x$	$2y - 5$
$10x + 1$	$y - 9$	$y + 1$	$y \div 10$
$y + \frac{1}{2}y$	$6x$	$10x + 3$	$30 - x$
$12x$	$5x + 3$	$5x + 2$	$y + 9$
$2x - 1$	$110 - y$	$3x + 5$	$\frac{1}{2}y$
$2x$	$2y - 15$	$y + 2$	First card

Note: Display Evaluating Expressions 2 Overhead Transparency (page 142) during this game.

I have the **first card.**

Who has 3x?

I have **51.**

Who has 5y – 3?

I have **45.**

Who has 4y – 7?

I have **57.**

Who has 5y – 1?

I have **41.**

Who has 6y – 2?

I have **59.**

Who has 5x + 1?

I have **70.**

Who has x + 10?

I have **76.**

Who has x + 1?

I have **25.**

Who has 2x + 21?

I have **16.**

Who has 7y + 2?

I have **86.**

Who has 3*y*?

I have **60.**

Who has ½*y*?

I have **36.**

Who has 3*x* + 10?

I have **6.**

Who has 5*x*?

I have **55.**

Who has 2*x* + 10?

I have **75.**

Who has 3*x* − 1?

I have **40.**

Who has 4*y* + 6?

I have **44.**

Who has 4*x* + 1?

I have **54.**

Who has 5*y*?

I have **61.**

Who has 8*y* − 1?

 # Evaluating Expressions 2: x = 15, y = 12

I have **95.**

Who has 4x – 7?

I have **31.**

Who has 5y + 5?

I have **53.**

Who has 5y – 10?

I have **65.**

Who has 3x + 1?

I have **50.**

Who has ⅓x?

I have **46.**

Who has y + 3?

I have **5.**

Who has 4y + 1?

I have **15.**

Who has 7y + 1?

I have **49.**

Who has 2x + 1?

I have **85.**

Who has 3x + 2?

I have **47.**

Who has $3x - 2$?

I have **26.**

Who has $4y$?

I have **43.**

Who has $4x + 6$?

I have **48.**

Who has $4x - 8$?

I have **66.**

Who has $2x + 12$?

I have **52.**

Who has $3y - 1$?

I have **42.**

Who has $5y - 4$?

I have **35.**

Who has $5y - 2$?

I have **56.**

Who has $2x - 4$?

I have **58.**

Who has the first card?

Evaluating Expressions 2

Directions: As your classmates identify the answers to the algebraic equations, write the numbers in the boxes. Start at the top and go from left to right.

x = 15	y = 12

									3

Write an algebraic equation in terms of *x* and *y* for the first and last numbers of each row in the table above. The first one has been done for you.

1. _____ 3*y* + 9 = 45 _____   5. _____

2. _____   6. _____

3. _____   7. _____

4. _____   8. _____

Evaluating Expressions 2 Overhead Transparency

Teacher directions: Copy this page on an overhead transparency. Display the transparency. Cover the entire page with a piece of paper. As a student reads his or her card, show the same equation to help those who need the visual image to solve algebraic equations. They are listed from left to right so you can move the paper below the row.

x = 15		y = 12	
3x	4y – 7	6y – 2	x + 10
2x + 21	5y – 3	5y – 1	5x + 1
x + 1	7y + 2	3y	3x + 10
2x + 10	4y + 6	5y	½y
5x	3x – 1	4x + 1	8y – 1
4x – 7	5y – 10	⅓x	4y + 1
2x + 1	5y + 5	3x + 1	y + 3
7y + 1	3x + 2	3x – 2	4x + 6
2x + 12	5y – 4	2x – 4	4y
4x – 8	3y – 1	5y – 2	First card

I Have, Who Has!: Math • 5–6 © 2006 Creative Teaching Press

Note: Display Evaluating Expressions 3 Overhead Transparency (page 148) during this game.

I have the **first card.**

Who has $y - 8$?

I have **11.**

Who has $5y + 1$?

I have **2.**

Who has $6y$?

I have **51.**

Who has $4y + 4$?

I have **60.**

Who has $x + 10$?

I have **44.**

Who has $9y + 2$?

I have **35.**

Who has $3x + 6$?

I have **92.**

Who has $2y - 2$?

I have **81.**

Who has $y + 1$?

I have **18.**

Who has $10y - 1$?

Evaluating Expressions 3: x = 25, y = 10

I have **99.**

Who has 9y?

I have **79.**

Who has 2x + 17?

I have **90.**

Who has 2x − 4?

I have **67.**

Who has 4y + 1?

I have **46.**

Who has x + 4?

I have **41.**

Who has 8y + 3?

I have **29.**

Who has 6y − 3?

I have **83.**

Who has 6y + 4?

I have **57.**

Who has 3x + 4?

I have **64.**

Who has 7y − 4?

I Have, Who Has? Math • 5–6 © 2006 Creative Teaching Press

Evaluating Expressions 3: x = 25, y = 10

I have **66.**

Who has $2y + 2$?

I have **54.**

Who has $6y - 4$?

I have **22.**

Who has $3x$?

I have **56.**

Who has $2x + 5$?

I have **75.**

Who has $7y + 2$?

I have **55.**

Who has $5y + 3$?

I have **72.**

Who has $y - 1$?

I have **53.**

Who has $9y - 2$?

I have **9.**

Who has $2x + 4$?

I have **88.**

Who has $2x - 3$?

I have **47**.

Who has 5y?

I have **36**.

Who has 2x – 5?

I have **50**.

Who has 2x + 8?

I have **45**.

Who has y + 3?

I have **58**.

Who has 4y + 3?

I have **13**.

Who has 6y + 5?

I have **43**.

Who has 8y – 4?

I have **65**.

Who has 2x – 2?

I have **76**.

Who has 3y + 6?

I have **48**.

Who has the first card?

Evaluating Expressions 3

Directions: As your classmates identify the answers to the algebraic equations, write the numbers in the boxes. Start at the top and go from left to right.

x = 25	y = 10

							250

Write an algebraic equation in terms of *x* and *y* for the first and last numbers of each row in the table above. The first one has been done for you.

1. _____ 2y – 18 = 2 _____

2. _____

3. _____

4. _____

5. _____

6. _____

7. _____

8. _____

Evaluating Expressions 3 Overhead Transparency

Teacher directions: Copy this page on an overhead transparency. Display the transparency. Cover the entire page with a piece of paper. As a student reads his or her card, show the same equation to help those who need the visual image to solve algebraic equations. They are listed from left to right so you can move the paper below the row.

x = 25		y = 10	
$y - 8$	$6y$	$x + 10$	$3x + 6$
$y + 1$	$5y + 1$	$4y + 4$	$9y + 2$
$2y - 2$	$10y - 1$	$9y$	$2x - 4$
$x + 4$	$6y - 3$	$3x + 4$	$2x + 17$
$4y + 1$	$8y + 3$	$6y + 4$	$7y - 4$
$2y + 2$	$3x$	$7y + 2$	$y - 1$
$2x + 4$	$6y - 4$	$2x + 5$	$5y + 3$
$9y - 2$	$2x - 3$	$5y$	$2x + 8$
$4y + 3$	$8y - 4$	$3y + 6$	$2x - 5$
$y + 3$	$6y + 5$	$2x - 2$	First card

I Have, Who Has?: Math • 5–6 © 2006 Creative Teaching Press

Evaluating Expressions 4: a = 10, b = 5

Note: Display Evaluating Expressions 4 Overhead Transparency (page 154) during this game.

I have the **first card.**

Who has 8a – 1?

I have **72.**

Who has 9a + 2?

I have **79.**

Who has 6a + 4?

I have **92.**

Who has 7a + 7?

I have **64.**

Who has a + 2?

I have **77.**

Who has 6a – 1?

I have **12.**

Who has 8a – 5?

I have **59.**

Who has 6a + 2?

I have **75.**

Who has 7a + 2?

I have **62.**

Who has 4a – 1?

I Have, Who Has?: Math • 5–6 © 2006 Creative Teaching Press

I have **39.**

Who has $5a + 2$?

I have **44.**

Who has $10b + 4$?

I have **52.**

Who has $2b - 1$?

I have **54.**

Who has $2a + 2$?

I have **9.**

Who has $7a + 4$?

I have **22.**

Who has $5b$?

I have **74.**

Who has $a - 9$?

I have **25.**

Who has $8a - 4$?

I have **1.**

Who has $4a + 4$?

I have **76.**

Who has $4a + 2$?

I Have, Who Has?: Math • 5-6 © 2006 Creative Teaching Press

I have **42.**

Who has 5*b* – 1?

I have **29.**

Who has 10*a* – 1?

I have **24.**

Who has 6*a* – 3?

I have **99.**

Who has 2*a* – 1?

I have **57.**

Who has 9*a* – 1?

I have **19.**

Who has 10*b* – 3?

I have **89.**

Who has 3*a* + 4?

I have **47.**

Who has 7*a* – 3?

I have **34.**

Who has 3*a* – 1?

I have **67.**

Who has 10*a*?

I have **100.**

Who has 5*a* – 1?

I have **27.**

Who has 10*a* – 9?

I have **49.**

Who has *b* – 3?

I have **91.**

Who has 7*b* + 2?

I have **2.**

Who has 2*b*?

I have **37.**

Who has 7*a* – 1?

I have **10.**

Who has 3*a* + 2?

I have **69.**

Who has 8*a* + 2?

I have **32.**

Who has 5*b* + 2?

I have **82.**

Who has the first card?

I Have, Who Has?: Math • 5–6 © 2006 Creative Teaching Press

Evaluating Expressions 4

Directions: As your classmates identify the answers to the algebraic equations, write the numbers in the boxes. Start at the top and go from left to right.

a = 10	b = 5

										500

Write an algebraic equation in terms of *a* and *b* for the first and last numbers of each row in the table above. The first one has been done for you.

1. _____ $10b + 29 = 79$ _____

2. _____

3. _____

4. _____

5. _____

6. _____

7. _____

8. _____

Evaluating Expressions 4 Overhead Transparency

Teacher directions: Copy this page on an overhead transparency. Display the transparency. Cover the entire page with a piece of paper. As a student reads his or her card, show the same equation to help those who need the visual image to solve algebraic equations. They are listed from left to right so you can move the paper below the row.

a = 10		b = 5	
$8a - 1$	$6a + 4$	$a + 2$	$8a - 5$
$7a + 2$	$9a + 2$	$7a + 7$	$6a - 1$
$6a + 2$	$4a - 1$	$5a + 2$	$2b - 1$
$7a + 4$	$a - 9$	$4a + 4$	$10b + 4$
$2a + 2$	$5b$	$8a - 4$	$4a + 2$
$5b - 1$	$6a - 3$	$9a - 1$	$3a + 4$
$3a - 1$	$10a - 1$	$2a - 1$	$10b - 3$
$7a - 3$	$10a$	$5a - 1$	$b - 3$
$2b$	$3a + 2$	$5b + 2$	$10a - 9$
$7b + 2$	$7a - 1$	$8a + 2$	First card

I Have, Who Has?: Math • 5–6 © 2006 Creative Teaching Press

Geometry Terms

I have the **first card.**

Who has the word for an exact location in space?

I have a **plane.**

Who has the word that describes two lines that intersect and form right angles?

I have a **point.**

Who has the word that names a line with one endpoint and another end that continues in one direction without end?

I have **perpendicular lines.**

Who has the word that names lines that cross at exactly one point?

I have a **ray.**

Who has the word for a part of a line that includes two endpoints and all of the points between them?

I have **intersecting lines.**

Who has the word for a closed plane figure formed by three or more line segments?

I have a **line segment.**

Who has the word for a figure formed by two rays that have a common endpoint?

I have a **polygon.**

Who has the word for a quadrilateral with opposite sides that are parallel and congruent?

I have an **angle.**

Who has the word for a flat surface that extends without end in all directions?

I have a **parallelogram.**

Who has the word for a parallelogram with four congruent sides?

I Have, Who Has? Math • 5–6 © 2006 Creative Teaching Press

Geometry Terms

I have a **rhombus.**

Who has the name of a triangle with two sides of the same length?

I have the **diameter.**

Who has the distance from the center of a circle to a point on the circle?

I have an **isosceles triangle.**

Who has the name of a triangle with sides that are all the same lengths?

I have the **radius.**

Who has the name of an angle that measures exactly 90°?

I have an **equilateral triangle.**

Who has the name of a triangle with sides that are different lengths?

I have a **right angle.**

Who has the name of an angle that measures less than 90°?

I have a **scalene triangle.**

Who has a line segment that connects two points on a curve?

I have an **acute angle.**

Who has the name of an angle that measures more than 90°?

I have the **chord.**

Who has a line segment with both endpoints on the circle and that passes through the center?

I have an **obtuse angle.**

Who has the name of an angle that measures exactly 180°?

I Have, Who Has?: Math • 5–6 © 2006 Creative Teaching Press

Geometry Terms

I have a **straight angle.**

Who has the name of two angles that create a 90° angle?

I have a **pentagon.**

Who has a polygon with nine sides?

I have **complementary angles.**

Who has the name of two angles that create a 180° angle?

I have a **nonagon.**

Who has a polygon with seven sides?

I have **supplementary angles.**

Who has the word that means having the same size and shape?

I have a **heptagon.**

Who has the word for a quadrilateral with one pair of parallel sides?

I have **congruent.**

Who has a polygon with ten sides?

I have a **trapezoid.**

Who has a polygon with twelve sides?

I have a **decagon.**

Who has a polygon with five sides?

I have a **dodecagon.**

Who has the word for the distance around a circle?

I Have, Who Has?: Math • 5–6 • © 2006 Creative Teaching Press

Geometry Terms

I have the **circumference.**

Who has the word for a plane formed by two intersecting and perpendicular number lines called axes?

I have an **ordered pair.**

Who has the word for a flat surface of a solid?

I have a **coordinate plane.**

Who has the word for the vertical number line on a coordinate plane?

I have a **face.**

Who has the word for a solid figure that has the shape of a round ball?

I have the **y-axis.**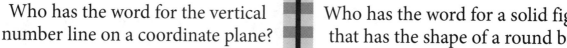

Who has the word for the horizontal number line on a coordinate plane?

I have a **sphere.**

Who has the word for lines that never intersect and are in the same plane?

I have the **x-axis.**

Who has the word for each of the four parts of a coordinate plane?

I have **parallel lines.**

Who has the word for a portion of the circumference of a circle?

I have a **quadrant.**

Who has the word for a pair of numbers used to locate a point on a coordinate plane?

I have an **arc.**

Who has the first card?

I Have, Who Has?: Math • 5–6 • © 2006 Creative Teaching Press

Geometry Terms

Directions: Follow the path by highlighting the geometry terms as your classmates identify them.

START ✪	tangent	equilateral triangle	square	parallel lines	FINISH ✪
point	isosceles triangle	cube	scalene triangle	sphere	arc
ray	sphere	rhombus	prism	chord	face
addend	line segment	parallelogram	diameter	quadrant	ordered pair
polygon	angle	polygon	radius	x-axis	circle
plane	perpendicular lines	intersecting lines	cylinder	right angle	y-axis
ratio	decagon	pentagon	obtuse angle	acute angle	coordinate plane
congruent	complementary angles	straight angle	nonagon	pyramid	circumference
supplementary angles	cone	plane	heptagon	trapezoid	dodecagon

Choose five words from the table above that you did **not** highlight. Write a definition for each word.

1. _____ = _____

2. _____ = _____

3. _____ = _____

4. _____ = _____

5. _____ = _____

Note: Display Coordinate Plane Overhead Transparency 1 (page 164) during this game.

I have the **first card.**

Who has the object located at coordinates (-4, 7)?

I have the **book.**

Who has the object located at coordinates (-5, 0)?

I have the **baseball.**

Who has the object located at coordinates (-3, -9)?

I have the **sock.**

Who has the object located at coordinates (3, -1)?

I have the **cactus.**

Who has the object located at coordinates (1, 5)?

I have the **flower.**

Who has the object located at coordinates (-7, 6)?

I have the **house.**

Who has the object located at coordinates (-1, -6)?

I have the **fish.**

Who has the object located at coordinates (-2, -2)?

I have the **hammer.**

Who has the object located at coordinates (-9, 5)?

I have the **triangle.**

Who has the object located at coordinates (-9, -9)?

I have the **bells.**

Who has the object located at coordinates (0, ⁻9)?

I have the **cup.**

Who has the object located at coordinates (⁻6, ⁻3)?

I have the **pizza.**

Who has the object located at coordinates (4, 4)?

I have the **gingerbread boy.**

Who has the object located at coordinates (3, 7)?

I have the **hand.**

Who has the object located at coordinates (⁻5, 9)?

I have the **crayon.**

Who has the object located at coordinates (2, ⁻8)?

I have the **dolphin.**

Who has the object located at coordinates (6, ⁻3)?

I have the **trophy.**

Who has the object located at coordinates (8, 0)?

I have the **pentagon.**

Who has the object located at coordinates (⁻7, ⁻7)?

I have the **star.**

Who has the object located at coordinates (0, 0)?

I have the **heart.**

Who has the object located at coordinates (0, 9)?

I have the **flag.**

Who has the object located at coordinates (1, ⁻4)?

I have the **turtle.**

Who has the object located at coordinates (8, 3)?

I have the **car.**

Who has the object located at coordinates (⁻8, 8)?

I have the **scissors.**

Who has the object located at coordinates (7, 9)?

I have the **raindrop.**

Who has the object located at coordinates (⁻9, ⁻3)?

I have the **leaf.**

Who has the object located at coordinates (9, 5)?

I have the **apple.**

Who has the object located at coordinates (6, 6)?

I have the **sun.**

Who has the object located at coordinates (⁻6, 3)?

I have the **money bag.**

Who has the object located at coordinates (4, ⁻5)?

I have the **glasses.**

Who has the object located at coordinates (⁻8, 1)?

I have the **umbrella.**

Who has the object located at coordinates (2, 1)?

I have the **plane.**

Who has the object located at coordinates (9, ⁻4)?

I have the **telephone.**

Who has the object located at coordinates (8, ⁻9)?

I have the **envelope.**

Who has the object located at coordinates (⁻3, 2)?

I have the **chick.**

Who has the object located at coordinates (5, ⁻7)?

I have the **hat.**

Who has the object located at coordinates (7, ⁻6)?

I have the **carrot.**

Who has the object located at coordinates (⁻3, 4)?

I have the **paintbrush.**

Who has the object located at coordinates (⁻4, ⁻5)?

I have the **arrow.**

Who has the first card?

I Have, Who Has?: Math • 5–6 © 2006 Creative Teaching Press

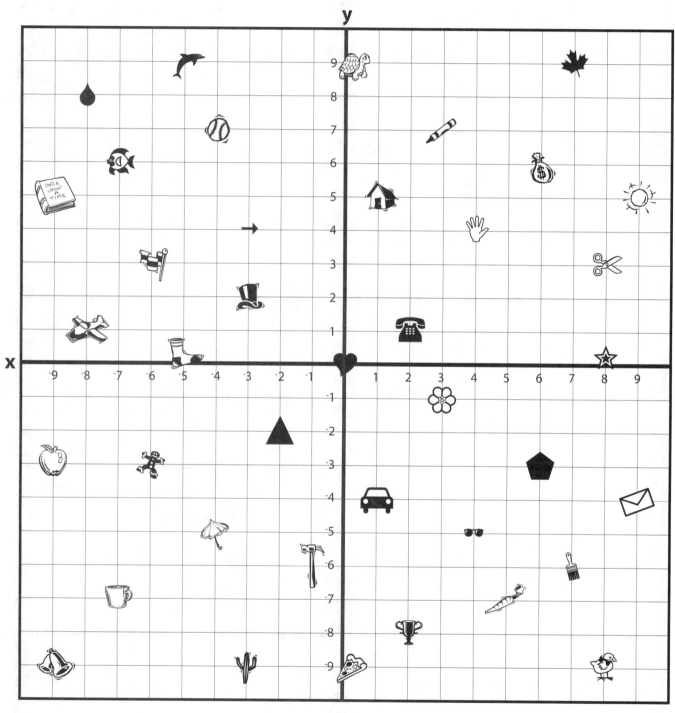

Note: Display Coordinate Plane Overhead Transparency 1 (page 164) during this game.

I have the **first card.**

Who has the x coordinate
for the crayon?

I have $x = 6$.

Who has the x coordinate
for the fish?

I have $x = 3$.

Who has the quadrant the fish is in?

I have $x = {}^-7$.

Who has the y coordinate
for the hand?

I have **quadrant 2 (II).**

Who has the x coordinate
for the glasses?

I have $y = 4$.

Who has the x coordinate
for the flag?

I have $x = 4$.

Who has the y coordinate
for the raindrop?

I have $x = {}^-6$.

Who has the y coordinate
for the hammer?

I have $y = 8$.

Who has the x coordinate
for the money bag?

I have $y = {}^-6$.

Who has the x coordinate
for the chick?

I have $x = 8$.

Who has the y coordinate for the plane?

I have $x = {}^-2$.

Who has the y coordinate for the carrot?

I have $y = 1$.

Who has the y coordinate for the house?

I have $y = {}^-7$.

Who has the x coordinate for the carrot?

I have $y = 5$.

Who has the x coordinate for the sock?

I have $x = 5$.

Who has the x coordinate for the bells?

I have $x = {}^-5$.

Who has the y coordinate for the flower?

I have $x = {}^-9$.

Who has the x coordinate for the sun?

I have $y = {}^-1$.

Who has the x coordinate for the triangle?

I have $x = 9$.

Who has the y coordinate for the trophy?

I Have, Who Has?: Math • 5–6 © 2006 Creative Teaching Press

I have $y = {}^-8$.

Who has the y coordinate for the pentagon?

I have $y = 3$.

Who has the y coordinate for the hat?

I have $y = {}^-3$.

Who has the x coordinate for the umbrella?

I have $y = 2$.

Who has the x coordinate for the telephone?

I have $x = {}^-4$.

Who has the y coordinate for the star?

I have $x = 2$.

Who has the x coordinate for the cactus?

I have $y = 0$.

Who has the x coordinate for the plane?

I have $x = {}^-3$.

Who has the quadrant the sun is in?

I have $x = {}^-8$.

Who has the y coordinate for the scissors?

I have **quadrant 1 (I)**.

Who has the y coordinate for the pizza?

I have $y = {}^-9$.

Who has the y coordinate for the leaf?

I have **quadrant 3 (III)**.

Who has the y coordinate for the car?

I have $y = 9$.

Who has the x coordinate for the hammer?

I have $y = {}^-4$.

Who has the y coordinate for the triangle?

I have $x = {}^-1$.

Who has the y coordinate for the fish?

I have $y = {}^-2$.

Who has the y coordinate for the baseball?

I have $y = 6$.

Who has the x coordinate for the paintbrush?

I have $y = 7$.

Who has the x coordinate for the heart?

I have $x = 7$.

Who has the quadrant the triangle is in?

I have $x = 0$.

Who has the first card?

I Have, Who Has?: Math • 5–6 © 2006 Creative Teaching Press

Coordinate Plane—Identify the Object at the Location 2

Note: Display Coordinate Plane Overhead Transparency 2 (page 173) during this game.

I have the **first card.**

Who has the object located at coordinates (⁻2, ⁻4)?

I have the **pentagon.**

Who has the object located at coordinates (1, ⁻9)?

I have the **chick.**

Who has the object located at coordinates (0, 6)?

I have the **cactus.**

Who has the object located at coordinates (⁻2, 4)?

I have the **pizza.**

Who has the object located at coordinates (2, ⁻6)?

I have the **dolphin.**

Who has the object located at coordinates (6, ⁻3)?

I have the **flower.**

Who has the object located at coordinates (8, 8)?

I have the **house.**

Who has the object located at coordinates (5, 9)?

I have the **triangle.**

Who has the object located at coordinates (⁻8, 3)?

I have the **leaf.**

Who has the object located at coordinates (⁻8, ⁻8)?

I have the **money bag.**

Who has the object located at coordinates (⁻3, 7)?

I have the **envelope.**

Who has the object located at coordinates (0, ⁻5)?

I have the **car.**

Who has the object located at coordinates (9, ⁻5)?

I have the **hammer.**

Who has the object located at coordinates (5, 6)?

I have the **pretzel.**

Who has the object located at coordinates (⁻6, 1)?

I have the **circle.**

Who has the object located at coordinates (⁻8, ⁻5)?

I have the **hand.**

Who has the object located at coordinates (9, ⁻1)?

I have the **telephone.**

Who has the object located at coordinates (⁻4, 9)?

I have the **umbrella.**

Who has the object located at coordinates (2, 1)?

I have the **scissors.**

Who has the object located at coordinates (⁻6, ⁻9)?

I Have, Who Has? Math • 5–6 © 2006 Creative Teaching Press

I have the **sock.**

Who has the object located at coordinates (⁻3, ⁻7)?

I have the **book.**

Who has the object located at coordinates (⁻1, 0)?

I have the **sun.**

Who has the object located at coordinates (2, 3)?

I have the **gingerbread boy.**

Who has the object located at coordinates (2, ⁻2)?

I have the **arrow.**

Who has the object located at coordinates (⁻3, ⁻2)?

I have the **trophy.**

Who has the object located at coordinates (⁻7, 8)?

I have the **heart.**

Who has the object located at coordinates (5, 0)?

I have the **carrot.**

Who has the object located at coordinates (⁻3, 2)?

I have the **baseball.**

Who has the object located at coordinates (⁻5, ⁻5)?

I have the **fish.**

Who has the object located at coordinates (6, 3)?

I have the **cup.**

Who has the object located at coordinates (⁻9, 6)?

I have the **hat.**

Who has the object located at coordinates (8, 5)?

I have the **flag.**

Who has the object located at coordinates (4, ⁻8)?

I have the **glasses.**

Who has the object located at coordinates (⁻9, ⁻2)?

I have the **star.**

Who has the object located at coordinates (9, 2)?

I have the **bells.**

Who has the object located at coordinates (2, 7)?

I have the **apple.**

Who has the object located at coordinates (8, ⁻7)?

I have the **raindrop.**

Who has the object located at coordinates (5, ⁻5)?

I have the **paintbrush.**

Who has the object located at coordinates (⁻6, 5)?

I have the **turtle.**

Who has the first card?

I Have, Who Has?: Math • 5–6 © 2006 Creative Teaching Press

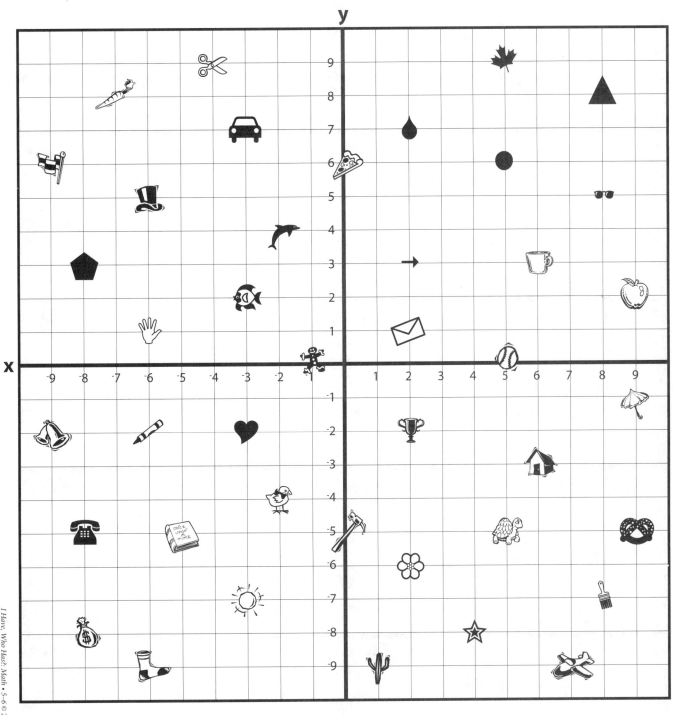

I have the **first card.**

Who has the quadrant the paintbrush is in?

I have $y = 5$.

Who has the y coordinate for the flower?

I have **quadrant 4 (IV).**

Who has the y coordinate for the fish?

I have $y = {}^-6$.

Who has the x coordinate for the carrot?

I have $y = 2$.

Who has the x coordinate for the triangle?

I have $x = {}^-7$.

Who has the x coordinate for the plane?

I have $x = 8$.

Who has the y coordinate for the chick?

I have $x = 7$.

Who has the y coordinate for the money bag?

I have $y = {}^-4$.

Who has the y coordinate for the hat?

I have $y = {}^-8$.

Who has the y coordinate for the raindrop?

I have $y = 7$.

Who has the x coordinate for the book?

I have $x = {}^-8$.

Who has the y coordinate for the gingerbread boy?

I have $x = {}^-5$.

Who has the y coordinate for the carrot?

I have $y = 0$.

Who has the x coordinate for the flag?

I have $y = 8$.

Who has the x coordinate for the arrow?

I have $x = {}^-9$.

Who has the x coordinate for the hat?

I have $x = 2$.

Who has the x coordinate for the scissors?

I have $x = {}^-6$.

Who has the y coordinate for the sun?

I have $x = {}^-4$.

Who has the x coordinate for the pentagon?

I have $y = {}^-7$.

Who has the y coordinate for the trophy?

I have $y = {}^-2$.

Who has the quadrant the circle is in?

I have $x = {}^-3$.

Who has the x coordinate for the apple?

I have **quadrant 1 (I)**.

Who has the y coordinate for the dolphin?

I have $x = 9$.

Who has the y coordinate for the scissors?

I have $y = 4$.

Who has the y coordinate for the umbrella?

I have $y = 9$.

Who has the x coordinate for the turtle?

I have $y = {}^-1$.

Who has the x coordinate for the bells?

I have $x = 5$.

Who has the x coordinate for the gingerbread boy?

I have $x = {}^-9$.

Who has the x coordinate for the heart?

I have $x = {}^-1$.

Who has the x coordinate for the star?

I Have, Who Has? Math • 5–6 © 2006 Creative Teaching Press

I have *x* = **4.**

Who has the quadrant
the book is in?

I have *y* = **6.**

Who has the *y* coordinate
for the envelope?

I have **quadrant 3 (III).**

Who has the *y* coordinate
for the house?

I have *y* = **1.**

Who has the *y* coordinate
for the pretzel?

I have *y* = **⁻3.**

Who has the *x* coordinate
for the cactus?

I have *y* = **⁻5.**

Who has the *x* coordinate
for the hammer?

I have *x* = **1.**

Who has the *y* coordinate
for the arrow?

I have *x* = **0.**

Who has the *y* coordinate
for the sock?

I have *y* = **3.**

Who has the *y* coordinate
for the flag?

I have *y* = **⁻9.**

Who has the first card?

Measurement Equivalents

I have the **first card.**

Who has the number of inches in a foot?

I have **24.**

Who has the number of fluid ounces in a cup?

I have **12.**

Who has the number of inches in a yard?

I have **8.**

Who has the number of quarts in a gallon?

I have **36.**

Who has the number of pennies in a dime?

I have **4.**

Who has the number of feet in a mile?

I have **10.**

Who has the number of centimeters in a meter?

I have **5,280.**

Who has the number of seconds in a minute?

I have **100.**

Who has the number of hours in a day?

I have **60.**

Who has the number of nickels in a dollar?

I Have, Who Has?. Math • © 2006 Creative Teaching Press

Measurement Equivalents

I have **20.**

Who has the number of cups in a pint?

I have **365.**

Who has the number of donuts in four dozen?

I have **2.**

Who has the number of weeks in a year?

I have **48.**

Who has the number of yards in a mile?

I have **52.**

Who has the number of years in a millennium?

I have **1,760.**

Who has the number of ounces in a pound?

I have **1,000.**

Who has the number of items in a baker's dozen?

I have **16.**

Who has the number of feet in a yard?

I have **13.**

Who has the number of days in a year?

I have **3.**

Who has the number of days in a week?

Measurement Equivalents

I have **7.**

Who has the number of
dimes in a half-dollar?

I have **6.**

Who has the number of
degrees of a line?

I have **5.**

Who has the number of
pounds in a ton?

I have **180.**

Who has the number of
degrees in a circle?

I have **2,000.**

Who has the number of
days in a leap year?

I have **360.**

Who has the number of
millimeters in 3 meters?

I have **366.**

Who has the number of
degrees in a right angle?

I have **3,000.**

Who has the number of
pints in 10 gallons?

I have **90.**

Who has the number of
sides on a hexagon?

I have **80.**

Who has the number of
quarters in ten dollars?

I Have, Who Has?: Math • 5–6 © 2006 Creative Teaching Press

Measurement Equivalents
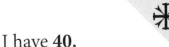

I have **40.**

Who has the number of
years in three decades?

I have **5,000.**

Who has the number of
cents in a half-dollar?

I have **30.**

Who has the number of
minutes in 2 hours?

I have **50.**

Who has the number of
seconds in 5 minutes?

I have **120.**

Who has the number of
decimeters in 15 meters?

I have **300.**

Who has the number of
cookies in twelve dozen?

I have **150.**

Who has the number of
months in 6 years?

I have **144.**

Who has the number of
cups in a half-pint?

I have **72.**

Who has the number of
grams in 5 kilograms?

I have **1.**

Who has the first card?

I Have, Who Has? Math • 5–6 © 2006 Creative Teaching Press

Measurement Equivalents

Directions: As your classmates identify the answers, draw a line to each number to complete the maze.

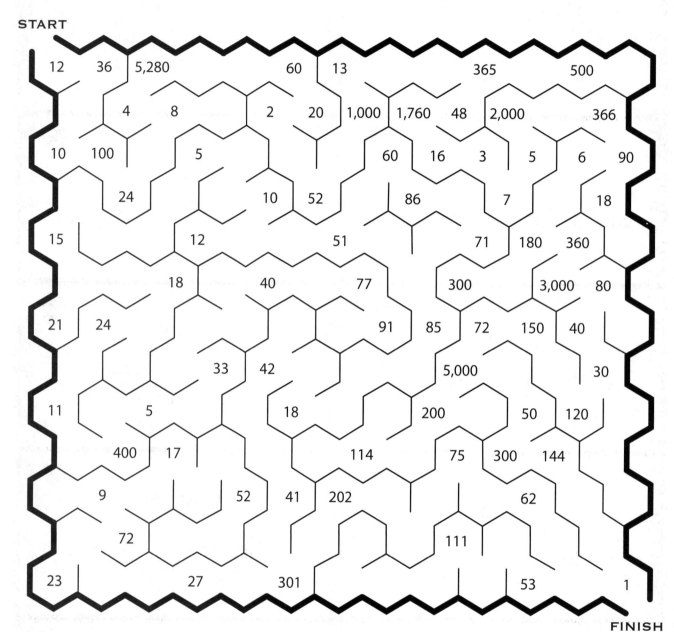

START

12   36   5,280   60   13   365   500

4   8   2   20   1,000   1,760   48   2,000   366

10   100   5   60   16   3   5   6   90

24   10   52   86   7   18

15   12   51   71   180   360

18   40   77   300   3,000   80

21   24   91   85   72   150   40

33   42   5,000   30

11   5   18   200   50   120

400   17   114   75   300   144

9   52   41   202   62

72   111

23   27   301   53   1

FINISH

I Have, Who Has?: Math • 5–6 © 2006 Creative Teaching Press

Circle Measurements

Note: Display Circle Measurements Overhead Transparency (page 187) during this game. Give each student a calculator.

I have the **first card.**

Who has the radius of Circle 1?

I have **94.2.**

Who has the radius of Circle 3?

I have **21.**

Who has the diameter of Circle 4?

I have **3.**

Who has the diameter of Circle 7?

I have **84.**

Who has the area of Circle 1?

I have **200.**

Who has the radius of Circle 5?

I have **1,384.74.**

Who has the radius of Circle 7?

I have **81.**

Who has the area of Circle 8?

I have **100.**

Who has the circumference of Circle 2?

I have **1,256.**

Who has the diameter of Circle 5?

I have **162.**

Who has the radius of Circle 2?

I have **200.96.**

Who has the radius of Circle 6?

I have **15.**

Who has the area of Circle 3?

I have **12.**

Who has the area of Circle 2?

I have **28.26.**

Who has the circumference of Circle 6?

I have **706.5.**

Who has the radius of Circle 4?

I have **75.36.**

Who has the diameter of Circle 6?

I have **42.**

Who has the area of Circle 7?

I have **24.**

Who has the area of Circle 9?

I have **31,400.**

Who has the circumference of Circle 10?

Circle Measurements

I have **25.12.**

Who has the diameter of Circle 2?

I have **5,538.96.**

Who has the radius of Circle 10?

I have **30.**

Who has the circumference of Circle 4?

I have **4.**

Who has the circumference of Circle 11?

I have **263.78.**

Who has the radius of Circle 8?

I have **87.92.**

Who has the diameter of Circle 3?

I have **20.**

Who has the circumference of Circle 12?

I have **6.**

Who has the circumference of Circle 9?

I have **31.4.**

Who has the area of Circle 4?

I have **50.24.**

Who has the radius of Circle 12?

Circle Measurements

I have **5.**

Who has the radius of Circle 9?

I have **14.**

Who has the circumference of Circle 7?

I have **8.**

Who has the circumference of Circle 3?

I have **628.**

Who has the area of Circle 6?

I have **18.84.**

Who has the diameter of Circle 11?

I have **452.16.**

Who has the diameter of Circle 12?

I have **28.**

Who has the circumference of Circle 1?

I have **10.**

Who has the area of Circle 12?

I have **131.88.**

Who has the radius of Circle 11?

I have **78.5.**

Who has the first card?

Circle Measurements
Overhead Transparency

r = radius	d = diameter	Π = 3.14
diameter = $2r$	circumference = Πd	area = Πr^2

1.
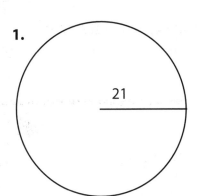
21

2.
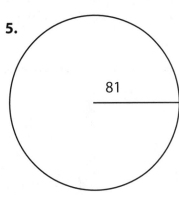
15

3.
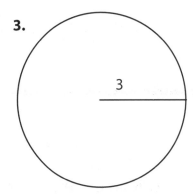
3

4.
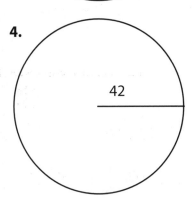
42

5.
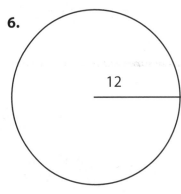
81

6.
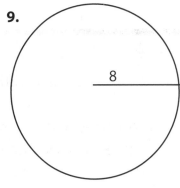
12

7.
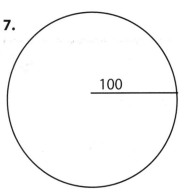
100

8.
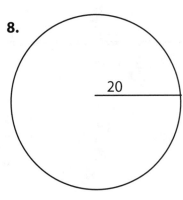
20

9.
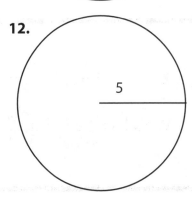
8

10.
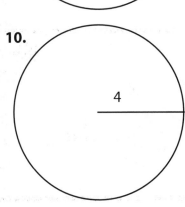
4

11.
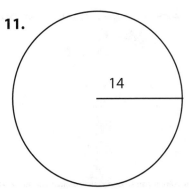
14

12.
5

Probability

Note: Display Probability Overhead Transparency (page 192) during this game.

I have the **first card.**

Who has the probability of picking a yellow marble?

I have **4:20.**

Who has the probability of picking a green or a purple marble?

I have **6:20.**

Who has the probability of picking a green marble?

I have **8:20.**

Who has the probability of picking a red or a green marble?

I have **3:20.**

Who has the probability of picking a black marble?

I have **7:20.**

Who has the probability of picking a purple or a red marble?

I have **1:20.**

Who has the probability of picking a purple marble?

I have **9:20.**

Who has the probability of picking a yellow or a purple marble?

I have **5:20.**

Who has the probability of picking a red marble?

I have **11:20.**

Who has the probability of picking a yellow or a red marble?

I have **10:20.**

Who has the color of the marbles that have the same probability of being picked?

I have **5:16.**

Who has the probability of spinning 8 on Spinner 2?

I have **white and black.**

Who has the color of the marble that has the greatest probability?

I have **6:16.**

Who has the probability of spinning 2 on Spinner 1?

I have **yellow.**

Who has the probability of spinning 1 on Spinner 1?

I have **1:8.**

Who has the probability of spinning 6 on Spinner 2?

I have **2:8.**

Who has the probability of spinning 3 on Spinner 1?

I have **2:16.**

Who has the probability of spinning 7 on Spinner 2?

I have **4:8.**

Who has the probability of spinning 5 on Spinner 2?

I have **3:16.**

Who has the probability of spinning 1 or 2 on Spinner 1?

Probability

I have **3:8.**

Who has the probability of spinning 5 or 6 on Spinner 2?

I have **6:8.**

Who has the probability of spinning 5 or 8 on Spinner 2?

I have **7:16.**

Who has the probability of spinning 6 or 8 on Spinner 2?

I have **11:16.**

Who has the number that has a 50% chance of being landed on for Spinner 1?

I have **8:16.**

Who has the probability of spinning 2 or 3 on Spinner 1?

I have **3.**

Who has the numbers that have the least probability of being landed on for Spinner 1?

I have **5:8.**

Who has the probability of spinning 7 or 8 on Spinner 2?

I have **2 and 4.**

Who has the number that has the greatest probability of being landed on for Spinner 2?

I have **9:16.**

Who has the probability of spinning 1 or 3 on Spinner 1?

I have **8.**

Who has the number that has the least probability of being landed on for Spinner 2?

I Have, Who Has?: Math • 5–6 © 2006 Creative Teaching Press

Probability

I have **6.**

Who has the number that has a 2:8 chance of being landed on?

I have **green.**

Who has the color of the marble that has a 5:20 chance of being chosen?

I have **1.**

Who has the number that has a 3:16 chance of being landed on?

I have **purple.**

Who has the color of the marble that has a 4:20 chance of being chosen?

I have **7.**

Who has the number that has a 5:16 chance of being landed on?

I have **red.**

Who has the number of marbles there are?

I have **5.**

Who has the number that has a 2:16 chance of being landed on?

I have **20.**

Who has the number of spaces on Spinner 2?

I have **6.**

Who has the color of the marble that has a 3:20 chance of being chosen?

I have **16.**

Who has the first card?

Probability Overhead Transparency

Marbles

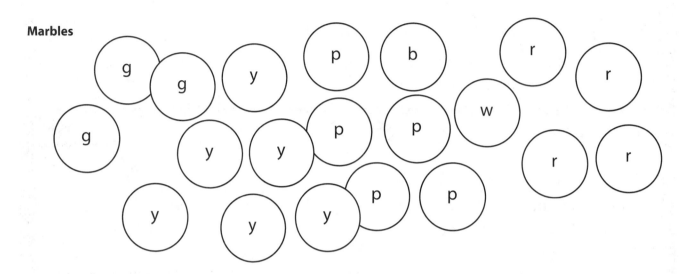

g = green   b = black   w = white
y = yellow   p = purple   r = red

Spinner 1

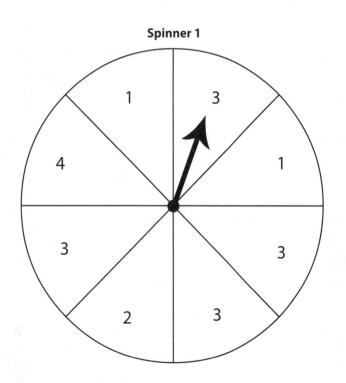

Spinner 2

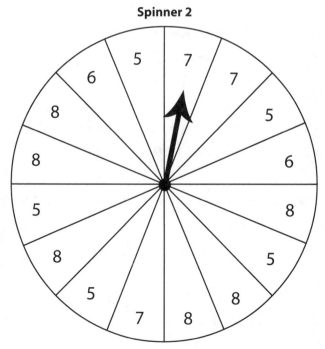

I Have, Who Has?: Math • 5–6 © 2006 Creative Teaching Press

Graphs

Note: Display Graphs Overhead Transparency (page 197) during this game.

I have the **first card.**

Who has the speed of the lion?

I have **30 mph.**

Who has the fastest animal?

I have **50 mph.**

Who has the speed of the rabbit?

I have the **cheetah.**

Who has the slowest animal?

I have **35 mph.**

Who has the speed of the cheetah?

I have the **elephant.**

Who has the animal that is half as fast as the cheetah?

I have **70 mph.**

Who has the speed of the elephant?

I have the **rabbit.**

Who has the animal that is 5 mph slower than a rabbit?

I have **25 mph.**

Who has the speed of the human?

I have the **human.**

Who has the animal that is 25 mph faster than an elephant?

Graphs

I have the **lion.**

Who has the difference of the cheetah's and the human's speeds?

I have **28.**

Who has the number of students in class on Thursday?

I have **40 mph.**

Who has the difference of the rabbit's and the elephant's speeds?

I have **26.**

Who has the number of students in class on Friday?

I have **10 mph.**

Who has the difference of the rabbit's and the lion's speeds?

I have **22.**

Who has the day that had the lowest attendance?

I have **15 mph.**

Who has the number of students in class on Monday?

I have **Friday.**

Who has the days that had the highest attendance?

I have **24.**

Who has the number of students in class on Tuesday?

I have **Tuesday and Wednesday.**

Who has the difference of the number of students who attended school on Monday and Tuesday?

I Have, Who Has?: Math • 5–6 © 2006 Creative Teaching Press

Graphs

I have **4.**

Who has the day that had 2 less students than Wednesday?

I have **40.**

Who has the number of students with brown hair?

I have **Thursday.**

Who has the day that had 4 less students than Tuesday?

I have **200.**

Who has the total number of students in the school?

I have **Monday.**

Who has the number of students with black hair?

I have **400.**

Who has the fraction of students with black hair?

I have **100.**

Who has the number of students with blonde hair?

I have **¼.**

Who has the percent of students with brown hair?

I have **60.**

Who has the number of students with red hair?

I have **50%.**

Who has the fraction of students with red hair?

Graphs

I have ¹/₁₀.

Who has the percent of students with black hair?

I have **blonde and red.**

Who has the hair color that is double the number of students with black hair?

I have **25%.**

Who has the percent of students who do not have black hair?

I have **brown.**

Who has the name of the graph that shows animals' speeds?

I have **75%.**

Who has the percent of students with red hair?

I have a **bar graph.**

Who has the name of the graph that shows hair color of students?

I have **10%.**

Who has the percent of students with blonde hair?

I have a **circle graph.**

Who has the name of the graph that shows class attendance?

I have **15%.**

Who has the two hair colors that equal the number of students with black hair?

I have a **line graph.**

Who has the first card?

I Have, Who Has?: Math • 5–6 © 2006 Creative Teaching Press

Graphs Overhead Transparency

Top Speeds of Animals

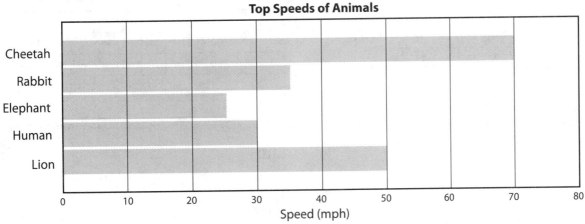

Cheetah
Rabbit
Elephant
Human
Lion

Speed (mph)

Grade 5 Class Attendance in One Week

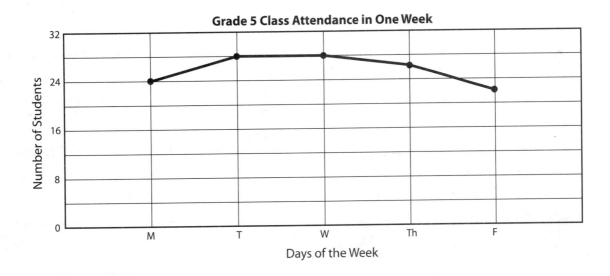

Number of Students

Days of the Week

Hair Color of Students in a School

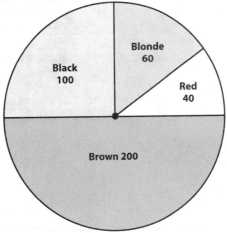

Black
100

Blonde
60

Red
40

Brown 200

Answer Key

Multiplication Review (Page 10)

90	28	121	21	63	49	44	100	72	54
22	24	27	108	36	55	81	48	60	110
96	56	42	77	120	99	33	70	66	144
132	35	45	84	15	10	88	50	25	1
1	2	3	4	5	6	7	8	9	10

1. 7
2. 11
3. 10
4. 5
5. 8
6. 9
7. 12
8. 5
9. 8
10. 11
11. 7
12. 8

Division Review (Page 15)

1	2	3	4	5	6	7	8	9	10
11	12	13	14	15	16	17	18	19	20
21	22	23	24	25	26	27	28	29	30
31	32	33	34	35	36	37	38	39	40
41	42	43	44	45	46	47	48	49	50
51	52	53	54	55	56	57	58	59	60
61	62	63	64	65	66	67	68	69	70
71	72	73	74	75	76	77	78	79	80
81	82	83	84	85	86	87	88	89	90
91	92	93	94	95	96	97	98	99	100

1. 15
2. 6
3. 4
4. 11
5. 4
6. 20
7. 4
8. 9
9. 7
10. 14
11. 11
12. 12

Basic Operations Mixed Review 1 (Page 20)

4	14	69	16	18	29	31	91	77	82	13
3	20	72	47	27	58	60	23	10	52	38
2	56	85	44	5	53	74	100	99	63	87
1	94	51	36	19	50	92	17	59	62	1
	A	B	C	D	E	F	G	H	I	J

1. 10
2. 25
3. 6
4. 120
5. 1
6. 35
7. 180
8. 4
9. 65
10. 8
11. 0
12. 11
13. 2
14. 5
15. 0
16. 472
17. 56
18. A2

Basic Operations Mixed Review 2 (Page 25)

Z	1	2	3	4	5	6	7	8	9	10
Y	11	12	13	14	15	16	17	18	19	20
X	21	22	23	24	25	26	27	28	29	30
W	31	32	33	34	35	36	37	38	39	40
V	41	42	43	44	45	46	47	48	49	50
U	51	52	53	54	55	56	57	58	59	60
T	61	62	63	64	65	66	67	68	69	70
S	71	72	73	74	75	76	77	78	79	80
R	81	82	83	84	85	86	87	88	89	90
Q	91	92	93	94	95	96	97	98	99	100
	A	B	C	D	E	F	G	H	I	J

1. DV 2. JU 3. BU 4. BX 5. JW 6. ES 7. EW 8. FT 9. HS 10. HV

Rounding Whole Numbers (Page 30)

30,000	4,900	500,000	7,000	21,600	3,100	3,400	5,600,000	4,400	20,000
9,000	3,900	1,000	37,100	60,000	3,310	800,000	70,000	410	4,200
2,000	460	5,000	600,000	2,500	1,700	12,000	3,200	15,000	3,500
90,000	50,000	1,500	4,000	1,900	70,000	900,000	100,000	1,400	1,600,000
4,100	4,800	3,000	8,000	800	700,000	65,000	95,000	300,000	7,000

1. 4,100 2. 60,000 3. 500,000
4. 5,000 5. 1,900 6. 700,000
7. 9,000 8. 90,000 9. 600,000
10. 4,800

Rounding Decimals to the Nearest Whole Number (Page 35)

1	2	3	4	5	6	7	8	9	10
11	12	13	14	15	16	17	18	19	20
21	22	23	24	25	26	27	28	29	30
31	32	33	34	35	36	37	38	39	40
41	42	43	44	45	46	47	48	49	50

1. 36 2. 42 3. 48 4. 23
5. 46 6. 47 7. 49 8. 41
9. 45 10. 43 11. 40 12. 90

Rounding Decimals to the Nearest Tenth (Page 40)

I	8.2	5.5	2.3	10.9	8.9	5.9	7.4	9.1	5.2	10.6
	L	L	C	R	A	C	U	T	A	O
II	2.5	6.5	7.1	2.1	3.5	8.5	6.2	2.2	3.2	3.3
	G	H	M	A	I	S	T	L	O	R
III	8.4	6.3	2.4	1.4	7.8	2.6	9.5	6.4	7.6	9.0
	E	I	Q	E	L	U	T	V	A	N
IV	2.6	7.7	8.7	3.9	5.7	2.9	7.3	1.5	1.3	1.0
	C	G	E	N	T	E	A	R	E	P

I	2.3	5.2	5.5	5.9	7.4	8.2	8.9	9.6	10.6	10.9
	C	A	L	C	U	L	A	T	O	R
II	2.1	2.2	2.5	3.2	3.3	3.5	6.2	6.5	7.1	8.5
	A	L	G	O	R	I	T	H	M	S
III	1.4	2.4	2.6	6.3	6.4	7.6	7.8	8.4	9.0	9.5
	E	Q	U	I	V	A	L	E	N	T
IV	1.0	1.3	1.5	1.6	2.9	3.9	5.7	7.3	7.7	8.7
	P	E	R	C	E	N	T	A	G	E

I. calculator
II. algorithms
III. equivalent
IV. percentage

Square Roots and Exponents— Numerical Format (Page 45)

Z	16	6	122	35	121	3	12	24	81	8
Y	15	4	7	5	82	25	99	9	26	64
X	20	10	36	27	48	15	63	19	11	101
W	17	2	50	144	49	37	145	65	100	22
	A	B	C	D	E	F	G	H	I	J

1. 4 2. 12 3. 7 4. 10
5. 4 6. 49 7. 27 8. 9
9. 8 10. 144 11. 11 12. 81

Square Roots and Exponents—Written Word Format (Page 50)

Z	4	17	81	99	1000	25	27	3	1	121
Y	50	9	5	16	26	125	12	19	101	8
X	6	120	10,000	82	0	54	7	10	18	37
W	62	2	35	13	11	37	49	28	17	44
	A	B	C	D	E	F	G	H	I	J

1. 36
2. 27
3. 11
4. 9
5. 121
6. 49
7. 5
8. 4
9. 8
10. 16
11. 7
12. 81
13. 16
14. 125
15. 1

Multiplying by an Exponent of Ten (Page 55)

200	30,000	1,400	9,200	500	800	3,400	400	1,500	1,300
51,000	6,300	300	47,000	8,000	2,000	900	12,000	50,000	700
600	9,000	60,000	1,100	1,700	5,000	1,600	3,000	1,200	90,000
6,000	4,000	15,000	7,000	13,000	30,000	14,000	40,000	900	*

1. 9×10^4
2. 2×10^2
Answers for 3–5 will vary.

Identifying Multiples and Factors (Page 60)

START	14 21 28	1, 12, 2, 6, 3, 4	40 60 80	100 200 300	1 25 5	30 45 60	1, 22, 2, 11	1, 75, 3, 25, 5, 15	1, 45, 3, 15, 3, 9
1, 16, 2, 8, 4	3 6 9	1, 24, 2, 12, 3, 8, 4, 6	5 10 15	1, 2, 10, 4, 5, 20	18 27 36	8 12 16	22 33 44	400 600 800	1, 10, 2, 5
1, 22, 2, 11	66, 99, 330	400 600 800	1, 33, 3, 11	25 50 75	1, 100, 2, 50, 4, 25, 5, 20, 10	14 21 28	8 16 24	1, 16, 2, 8, 4	1, 14, 2, 7
1, 30, 2, 15, 3, 10, 5, 6	32 48 64	60 90 120	22 33 44	1, 30, 2, 15, 3, 10, 5, 6	12 24 36	32 48 64	1, 60, 2, 30, 3, 20, 4, 15, 5, 12, 6, 10	1, 50, 2, 25, 5, 10	30 60 90
1, 40, 2, 20, 4, 10, 5, 8	6 12 18	10 20 30	1, 36, 2, 18, 3, 12, 4, 9, 6	20 40 60	1, 14, 2, 7	32 48 64	1, 35, 5, 7	40 60 80	66, 99, 330
1, 50, 2, 25, 5, 10	50 100 150	1, 12, 2, 6, 3, 4	1, 18, 2, 9, 3, 6	15 30 45	1 3 9	4 8 12	1, 45, 3, 15, 5, 9	1, 16, 2, 8, 4	FINISH

Answers for 1–5 will vary.

Least Common Multiple and Greatest Common Factor (Page 65)

START	24	40	30	48	20	10	60	42	6
	R	W	H	O	E	N	I	X	B
36	18	35	28	55	21	44	64	72	25
E	K	T	U	I	M	C	J	H	S
144	7	9	12	2	5	11	22	3	15
U	S	F	Y	I	A	R	J	Z	J
4	13	14	1	16	8	17	50	19	100
N	R	O	W	U	Y	F	A	N	R

NUMBERS	40	30	20	10	60	35	55	25	5	15	50	100
LETTERS	W	H	E	N	I	T	I	S	A	J	A	R

Riddle answer: When it is a jar.

Equivalent Fractions (Page 70)

2/18	20/55	10/16	5/30	88/121	6/21	2/30	20/100	20/150	10/14
16/28	5/60	50/100	49/77	70/100	10/110	80/100	60/144	60/90	25/55
12/28	20/110	6/20	75/100	33/121	25/100	8/22	60/100	81/99	10/100
2/6	30/33	5/40	30/55	18/20	40/100	35/42	8/30	9/63	5/7

1. 2/18 2. 10/14
3. 16/28 4. 25/55
5. 12/28 6. 10/100
7. 2/6 8. 9/63

Equivalents for the fractions will vary.

Reducing Fractions (Page 75)

9/10	5/7	2/3	11/25	1/2	3/8	1/10	3/7	3/5	2/9
4/25	1/4	2/5	1/8	4/5	5/6	2/7	3/10	1/3	1/12
1/25	4/9	1/5	3/4	1/6	1/7	1/15	7/10	5/8	6/7
1/9	2/15	5/12	8/9	1/13	7/8	4/7	7/12	5/9	3/8

1. 9/10 2. 2/9 3. 4/25 4. 1/12
5. 1/25 6. 6/7 7. 1/9 8. 5/9

Equivalents for the fractions will vary.

Changing Improper Fractions to Mixed Numbers (Page 80)

8 1/11	8 5/6	3 3/4	3 4/5	2 1/8	4 17/50	3 1/2	8 1/11	FINISH
2 1/2	10 1/3	3 3/8	6 1/2	7 2/3	2 6/25	12 1/3	10 1/3	3 1/2
2 1/5	4 1/2	2 3/10	3 3/4	9 2/7	2 1/18	3 1/4	7 2/7	10 1/3
3 1/3	2 1/5	2 1/6	5 1/3	6 2/3	3 1/2	2 1/5	4 1/4	3 1/12
2 1/2	6 1/4	4 2/3	5 1/6	3 4/5	3 2/11	12 1/3	2 1/8	8 1/12
3 1/3	7 1/11	12 5/12	4 1/11	7 3/4	5 1/2	8 1/4	11 2/3	5 1/3
START	8 1/6	6 1/10	11 1/3	12 2/3	5 1/2	8 5/6	7 1/10	4 1/2

Answers for 1–15 will vary.

Changing Mixed Numbers to Improper Fractions (Page 85)

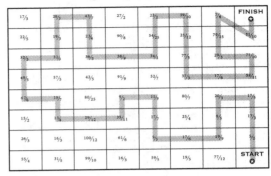

Answers for 1–15 will vary.

Changing Decimals to Percents (Page 90)

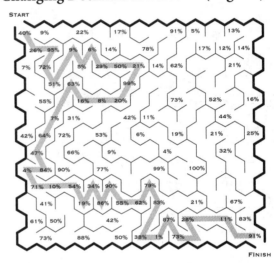

Changing Percents to Decimals (Page 95)

0.01	0.02	0.03	0.04	0.05	0.06	0.07	0.08	0.09	0.10
0.11	0.12	0.13	0.14	0.15	0.16	0.17	0.18	0.19	0.20
0.21	0.22	0.23	0.24	0.25	0.26	0.27	0.28	0.29	0.30
0.31	0.32	0.33	0.34	0.35	0.36	0.37	0.38	0.39	0.40
0.41	0.42	0.43	0.44	0.45	0.46	0.47	0.48	0.49	0.50
0.51	0.52	0.53	0.54	0.55	0.56	0.57	0.58	0.59	0.60
0.61	0.62	0.63	0.64	0.65	0.66	0.67	0.68	0.69	0.70
0.71	0.72	0.73	0.74	0.75	0.76	0.77	0.78	0.79	0.80
0.81	0.82	0.83	0.84	0.85	0.86	0.87	0.88	0.89	0.90
0.91	0.92	0.93	0.94	0.95	0.96	0.97	0.98	0.99	1.00

Answers for 2–12 will vary.

Changing Percents to Ratios (Page 100)

2:100	1:100	95:100	3:10	12:100	50:100	FINISH ✪
39:100	27:100	9:100	18:100	7:100	2:5	91:100
35:100	29:100	4:5	1:10	6:100	62:100	15:100
14:100	23:100	1:2	92:100	29:100	68:100	1:5
59:100	7:10	81:100	2:5	24:100	8:10	21:100
3:100	9:100	53:100	17:100	3:5	88:100	83:100
61:100	19:100	21:100	8:100	1:4	5:100	71:100
86:100	3:5	1:10	3:4	34:100	9:10	22:100
START ✪	49:100	1:2	7:10	97:100	81:100	3:4

Answers for 2–10 will vary.

Changing Ratios to Percents (Page 105)

1%	2%	3%	4%	5%	6%	7%	8%	9%	10%
11%	12%	13%	14%	15%	16%	17%	18%	19%	20%
21%	22%	23%	24%	25%	26%	27%	28%	29%	30%
31%	32%	33%	34%	35%	36%	37%	38%	39%	40%
41%	42%	43%	44%	45%	46%	47%	48%	49%	50%
51%	52%	53%	54%	55%	56%	57%	58%	59%	60%
61%	62%	63%	64%	65%	66%	67%	68%	69%	70%
71%	72%	73%	74%	75%	76%	77%	78%	79%	80%
81%	82%	83%	84%	85%	86%	87%	88%	89%	90%
91%	92%	93%	94%	95%	96%	97%	98%	99%	100%

Answers for 1–10 will vary.

Comparing Integers (Page 110)

	A	B	C	D	E	F	G	H	I	J
4	8	-9	-14	5	32	-42	16	-19	-87	21
3	-23	13	-20	66	6	-14	46	-5	35	-51
2	-10	47	98	26	-2	-29	-7	70	-45	-48
1	-62	-33	-12	-62	4	-37	57	100	-72	0

1. $-9 + -2 = -11$
2. $70 - -33 = 103$
3. $8 + -19 = -11$
4. $-20 - -72 = 52$
5. $26 - -7 = 33$
6. $-10 + 66 = 56$
7. $70 - 35 = 35$
8. $-42 - 57 = -99$
9. $21 + -51 = -30$
10. $13 - -14 = 27$
11. $-7 + 6 = -1$
12. $8 - -12 = 20$
13. $-2 + 100 = 98$
14. $5 + -5 = 0$
15. $-29 - -23 = -6$

Math Terminology (Page 115)

START ✪	AREA	VENN DIAGRAM	EXPANDED FORM	FRACTION	MEASUREMENT	FINISH ✪
MASS	PERIMETER	DIVISION	RANGE	GEOMETRY	DEGREES CELSIUS	DEGREES FAHRENHEIT
COMPOSITE NUMBER	VOLUME	ADDITION	FORMULA	EXPONENT	FACTOR	EQUATION
QUOTIENT	NUMBER LINE	ABSOLUTE VALUE	NUMERATOR	PROBABILITY	RATIO	DIVIDEND
POSITIVE NUMBERS	DENOMINATOR	ESTIMATE	SURFACE AREA	HISTOGRAM	SQUARE NUMBER	ALGEBRA
BAR GRAPH	PRODUCT	NEGATIVE NUMBERS	GREATEST COMMON FACTOR OR GCF	LINE GRAPH	EQUIVALENT	MULTIPLICATION
CIRCLE GRAPH	LEAST COMMON MULTIPLE OR LCM	MEAN	INTERSECT	MODE	CAPACITY	IMPROPER FRACTION
MIXED NUMBER	DIFFERENCE	PRIME NUMBER	PERCENT	DECIMAL	INTEGERS	CONGRUENT

The definitions will vary but must make sense and be accurate.

Extreme Mental Math (Page 120)

Answers for 1–3 will vary.

Absolute Value and Addition/Subtraction of Integers (Page 125)

1	-2	-10	37	72	-4	-15	62	13	-22
T	N	V	R	S	E	D	E	U	A
-1	6	8	-25	12	2	20	19	4	24
A	R	M	W	E	T	O	L	E	N
3	-20	7	-30	26	-8	21	0	-27	15
M	N	A	M	R	E	E	Y	O	K
22	-5	-7	5	30	25	31	-17	-13	12
I	E	T	C	E	V	S	D	E	T

-22	-15	-10	-4	-2	1	13	37	62	72
A	D	V	E	N	T	U	R	E	S
-25	-1	2	4	6	8	12	19	20	24
W	A	T	E	R	M	E	L	O	N
-30	-27	-20	-8	0	3	7	15	21	26
M	O	N	E	Y	M	A	K	E	R
-17	-13	-7	-5	5	12	22	25	30	31
D	E	T	E	C	T	I	V	E	S

Four ten-letter words: adventures, watermelon, moneymaker, detectives

Number Patterns (Page 130)

59	35	-12	-20	54	42	57	FINISH
100	-5	0	16	8	3	58	10,000
89	13	25	1,000	60	73	30	240
50	-4	24	39	21	55	81	2
20	200	29	36	333	90	256	88
44	15	75	243	105	91	83	34
5	10	49	71	400	39	46	7
START	67	45	48	33	-1	-9	400

Patterns will vary.

Evaluating Expressions 1 (Page 135)

79	26	88	49	6	76	92	20	99	13
53	58	2	72	50	86	9	90	28	95
81	41	51	5	75	48	83	22	96	43
42	59	15	60	29	25	16	85	52	100

Answers for 2–8 will vary.

Evaluating Expressions 2 (Page 141)

45	41	70	25	51	57	59	76	16	86
36	55	40	54	60	6	75	44	61	95
53	50	5	49	31	65	46	15	85	47
43	66	42	56	26	48	52	35	58	3

Answers for 2–8 will vary.

Evaluating Expressions 3 (page 147)

2	60	35	81	11	51	44	92	18	99
90	46	29	57	79	67	41	83	64	66
22	75	72	9	54	56	55	53	88	47
50	58	43	76	36	45	13	65	48	250

Answers for 2–8 will vary.

Evaluating Expressions 4 (page 153)

79	64	12	75	72	92	77	59	62	39
52	9	74	1	44	54	22	25	76	42
24	57	89	34	29	99	19	47	67	100
49	2	10	32	27	91	37	69	82	500

Answers for 2–8 will vary.

Geometry Terms (Page 159)

START	TANGENT	EQUILATERAL TRIANGLE	SQUARE	PARALLEL LINES	FINISH
POINT	ISOSCELES TRIANGLE	CUBE	SCALENE TRIANGLE	SPHERE	ARC
RAY	SPHERE	RHOMBUS	PRISM	CHORD	FACE
ADDEND	LINE SEGMENT	PARALLELOGRAM	DIAMETER	QUADRANT	ORDERED PAIR
POLYGON	ANGLE	POLYGON	RADIUS	X-AXIS	CIRCLE
PLANE	PERPENDICULAR LINES	INTERSECTING LINES	CYLINDER	RIGHT ANGLE	Y-AXIS
RATIO	DECAGON	PENTAGON	OBTUSE ANGLE	ACUTE ANGLE	COORDINATE PLANE
CONGRUENT	COMPLEMENTARY ANGLES	STRAIGHT ANGLE	NONAGON	PYRAMID	CIRCUMFERENCE
SUPPLEMENTARY ANGLES	CONE	PLANE	HEPTAGON	TRAPEZOID	DODECAGON

The definitions will vary but must make sense and be accurate.

Measurement Equivalents (Page 182)

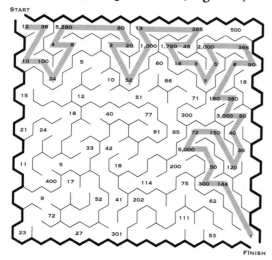

204

Notes

Notes